We dedicate this book to all lovers of the "Summer Game". To all our friends, past and present, with whom we have crossed bats (and pens), and to our dear friends Brian and Marion Littlewood, who have given us so much support and friendship over many seasons.

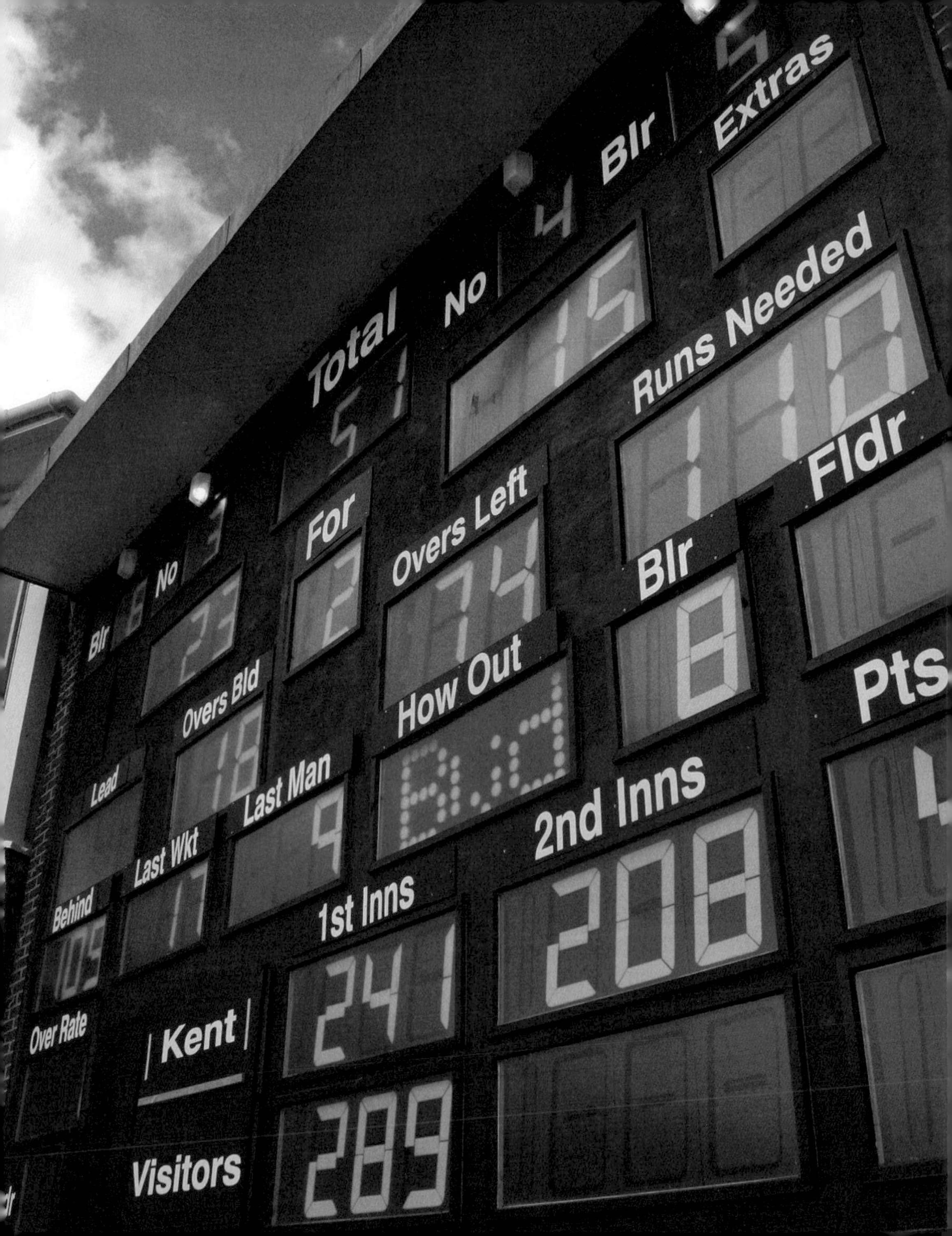

Blr   Extras

Total   No   4   5

51   15   **Runs Needed** 110

Fldr

For   **Overs Left**   **Blr**

Blr No   2   74   8

23   **Overs Bld**   **How Out**   **Pts**

18   6.3

Lead **Last Man** 9   **2nd Inns**

Behind **Last Wkt** 17 **1st Inns** 208

105

Over Rate **Kent** 241

Visitors 289

WITHDRAWN FROM
BROMLEY LIBRARIES

The Game of
Cricket

The Game of Cricket

Published by:
Greatest Guides Limited, Woodstock, Bridge End, Warwick
CV34 6PD, United Kingdom

www.greatestguides.com

Illustrations by Graham Kennedy and Bill Far.

Greatest Guides is committed to a sustainable future for our
planet. This book is printed on paper certified by the Forest
Stewardship Council.

FSC FSC® C020837
MIX
Paper

Printed and bound in the United Kingdom

ISBN 978-1-907906-14-5

Contents

Foreword from Dennis Amiss…

It gave me great pleasure to be asked to write the foreword to *The Game of Cricket*. I am not sure how qualified I am to do this as I was mainly a batsman and therefore do not know much, for instance, about bowling or wicketkeeping. During my career, however, I thought I knew a little about fielding in all positions, although some who saw me in my later years, including one or two Warwickshire players, maybe wouldn't agree! In my early years, though, I thought I had both pace across the ground as well as an accurate arm for return to the keeper or bowler.

As a batsman, there is a tip of my own I would like to give you – put everything out of your mind and focus hard on the bowler's hand at the moment he releases the ball. This will help you to pick up the ball early and tell you whether to come forward or play back. Also watch Ricky Ponting. He had the best batting technique of any player in the world. Watch his first trigger movement, where his feet and head are and where his bat is at the moment the ball is released from the bowler's hand. You can't go wrong if you practise this but it must first of all be in the nets.

Anyway, this is a marvellous book with splendid cricketing tips for all ages – players and fans – and should be always kept either in the cricketer's bag or in the coat pocket.
It covers all areas of the game from playing to umpiring, scoring and groundsmanship. There is something here for every cricketing player and fan of the game. I promise you, when reading this book you will often say to yourself "Well, I didn't know that!"

Good luck and best wishes for a successful season.

Dennis Amiss MBE

" To me, it doesn't matter how good you are. Sport is all about playing and competing. Whatever you do in cricket and in sport, enjoy it, be positive and try to win. "

Ian Botham

Part One
Playing Cricket

Chapter 1

The Game

AIMS OF THE GAME

Even in this day and age, cricket, whether it is a friendly, league, cup or evening limited-over game, is a game played in a competitive but gentlemanly manner! The game of cricket is played worldwide, and gives enjoyment to men and women, boys and girls of all races and creeds, participants and spectators alike. At grass roots level, there is a camaraderie between players who see each other maybe only twice a year; and stories are told about previous encounters, legendary characters of the game, cricket stories from days gone by, all taking precedence over the troubles of the day and of course that dreaded subject – the football season.

This wonderful game of cricket in all its different forms is based upon laws (not rules!) which are set by the game's governing body, the ECB (the England and Wales Cricket Board).

WHAT IS CRICKET?

Basically the game of cricket is contested between two teams of eleven players. The game is officiated by two umpires and recorded by two scorers. One side bats first, against the other side's bowling and fielding, accumulating a number of runs in a set amount of 'overs'. The roles are then reversed, with the side who bowled first trying to overhaul the other side's total of runs with their batting. Each side's total of runs is called an 'innings'.

OR ... THE DEFINITION OF CRICKET AS EXPLAINED TO A FOREIGNER

You have two sides, one out in the field and one in. Each man that's in the side that's in goes out, and when he's out he comes in and the next man goes in until he's out.

When they are all out, the side that's out comes in and the side that's been in goes out and tries to get those coming in, out. Sometimes you get men still in and not out.

When a man goes out to go in, the men who are out try to get him out, and when he is out he goes in and the next man in goes out and goes in. There are two men called umpires who stay out all the time and they decide when the men who are in are out.

When both sides have been in and all the men have been out, and both sides have been out twice after all the men have been in, including those who are not out, that is the end of the game! Simple!

HOW IS IT PLAYED?

At all times there are two batsmen, one at each end of the wicket. A bowler bowls six legitimate balls at a time (hopefully) and these are collectively called an 'over'. At the end of each over another bowler starts to bowl from the opposite end. This continues until the requisite number of overs has been bowled by the fielding side.

PARTS OF A CRICKET GROUND

A cricket field can be divided into three parts – infield, close-infield, outfield.

Infield – The infield is made by drawing an arc of 30 yards radius from the centre to each wicket with respect to the breadth of the pitch. The two arcs are then joined by parallel lines which are at a distance of 30 yards from the centre of the pitch with respect to the length of the pitch.

Close-infield – The close-infield is defined by drawing a circle of radius 15 yards from the centre of each wicket.

Outfield – The part of the ground which is on the outer side of the infield is termed the outfield.

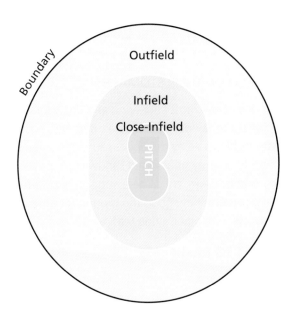

HOW DO YOU SCORE RUNS?

To score 'runs', the batsman has to hit the ball into spaces between the fielders and run to the other end of the wicket. Once both batsmen have reached their opposite end of the wicket, they have completed a run. Should the batsman hit the ball hard enough to cross the boundary (the perimeter of the playing field) they will have scored four runs, and if the boundary has been cleared without the ball touching the ground, they will have scored six runs.

IS THAT ALL?

Oh dear me no. The bowler's aim is to beat the batsman's bat and hit the wickets, the batsman is then dismissed ('bowled out') and replaced by the next batsman. Should the batsman hit the ball in the air and have the misfortune to be caught by a fielder before the ball touches the ground, then he is dismissed by being 'caught out'. There are other ways in which a batsman can be out, these are just the basics, but this does give a simple guideline as to how this wonderful game is played.

CLUB TEAMS MARCH ON THEIR STOMACHS!

You will find that one of the most endearing and enjoyable aspects of the game of cricket is the famous 'cricket tea'. Between hostilities on the field of play, it is possible to enjoy the endeavours of the tea ladies (sorry – tea persons), and their array of assorted sandwiches, pastas, hot potato wedges, quiches, pizzas, cakes, trifles, tea, and squash. Sorry if I'm getting carried away, but no matter how good the ground, or amenable the facilities, teams always remember a fine tea!

FROM GRASSROOTS TO FIRST CLASS

Cricket is played at many levels. Grassroots cricket is played throughout this country – village and club teams who only play friendly fixtures, leading to those who play in leagues. Many of these are 'feeder' leagues from which teams can progress to the highest status in their respective counties, such as the Lancashire or Yorkshire leagues, from which the majority of professional cricketers who represent their county learn their skills. A great number of these grassroots clubs provide the backbone of junior cricket which, together with some schools, give qualified coaching and match experience to youngsters from the age of nine upwards. In these nurseries they can spot young talent, who can then progress to play at county level in their own age groups.

EARLY DOORS

So, where and when can you start to play cricket? 'Kwik Cricket' is played by children from the age of 5 years old at participating schools and cricket clubs. Soundly based on the cricket game, but using brightly coloured plastic stumps and bats, both boys and girls can learn their hand and eye coordination skills – but with a soft ball at this stage!

HELPING HANDS

Junior cricket from Under 9's through to Under 18's is played at many cricket clubs, who have men and women 'coaches'. These people, mostly dedicated volunteers, have passed exams to teach youngsters how to play the game of cricket. With their expertise they are able to coach junior players in all aspects of the game – batting, bowling and fielding.

JOIN THE CLUB

Wherever you live, you can be sure that a cricket club is not too far away, and to use their facilities you will need to become a member. There will be a nominal annual fee, and a match fee for each game you play to cover the cost of teas and refreshments.

Maintaining a clubhouse and cricket field, as everything in life, costs money, and clubs are managed by the members themselves. Each club will have a few dedicated members who are responsible for such things as pitch preparation, finances, fund raising, organising fixtures and team selections.

I myself, have been lucky enough to have been able to donate my time over the years, ranging from junior representative on the committee, to club secretary, club groundsman and even captain on several occasions.

PLAYING WITH THE BIG BOYS

As junior players get older – and bigger, they should get the chance to play in adult cricket matches. This is all part of a learning curve, and a lot can be gained by watching older, more experienced players.

I recall playing as a raw 15 year old, batting at number 6 for the 1ˢᵗ XI, hitting a ball that went screaming through the air over a tall, but in my eyes very old, fielder, who jumped and plucked the ball out of the air with the greatest of ease. As I sulked back to the changing room, my captain told me that I had just been caught by a 55 year old ex England goalkeeper, and I should have hit the ball along the ground!

EYE OF THE TIGER

Some years ago, both myself and Roly were members of a well renowned club in Staffordshire that boasted strong sides both in batting and bowling. On one particular afternoon, with the visitors in the field after tea, our own team was playing with a junior member as the number 11 bat.

With four overs left to play our young number 11 came out to the crease. He would have been about ten years old I believe and the sight of him in his whites and very copious sweater I shall always remember. His cap was on his head at exactly the right angle and his bat appeared as large as himself.

The bowler bowled the ball at considerably less than his normal attack. The ball was graceful and approached our young bat with delivered ease. Then, with his face set determinedly, our young number 11 struck. The ball sailed for 4! The next two balls were all similarly despatched and the bowler ruefully smiled at the young batsman who continued to bat until the end of the innings when he left the field to great applause and I expect great respect from the visitors.

This young man now plays for Nottinghamshire!

GOING FOR A BREAK

Many cricket clubs organise a few days playing cricket in other parts of the country, or in some cases abroad. This is the Annual Cricket Tour, an experience not to be missed. Generally a trip taken between Monday and Friday, so that the week-end's cricket fixtures are not missed.

Both my esteemed co-author Roly and I have been on tour to Somerset and North Devon for the past 20 years, and we still enjoy a good old West Country welcome wherever the games are played – and of course the cider!

Before the start of this season, I was privileged to go on a 17 day tour to India with the Bournemouth Wanderers – 8 games of cricket and wonderful sight-seeing trips on the rest days. It was wonderful to experience the Indian culture, hospitality and the heat!

TWENTY 20 CRICKET

Whether a cricket fan or not, everyone has heard of this, the most recent phenomenon to have come to the professional game, both at county and international levels. This show-biz style and fast moving version of cricket has great entertainment value, capturing the eye of the public young and old.

But 20 over, and other shortened formats of the game have been played for many years, whether in a league or knock-out form. Indeed, the longest running 20 over knock-out competition, the Chauntrey Cup, has been held annually at Lichfield Cricket Club uninterrupted, even throughout the war years, since 1935.

THE LATTER YEARS

So far we have started at 5 years old, progressed through the junior age groups on to adult cricket. So where does it finish? Provided that you stay fairly fit, and still possess that 'buzz' whenever you put on those cricket whites, you can play indefinitely! And there are still honours to be won too. There is 45 over competitive cricket played between the counties at over 50, over 60 and even over 70s, and although these players are not as fleet of foot as in their earlier years, and the physiques may appear a little more portly, there is still a lot of skill on show and of course that desire to win!

As a lifelong cricketer, it has been my honour to have played for several seasons in the Hampshire Over 50s, playing alongside and against some very talented cricketers, some of whom have international honours too.

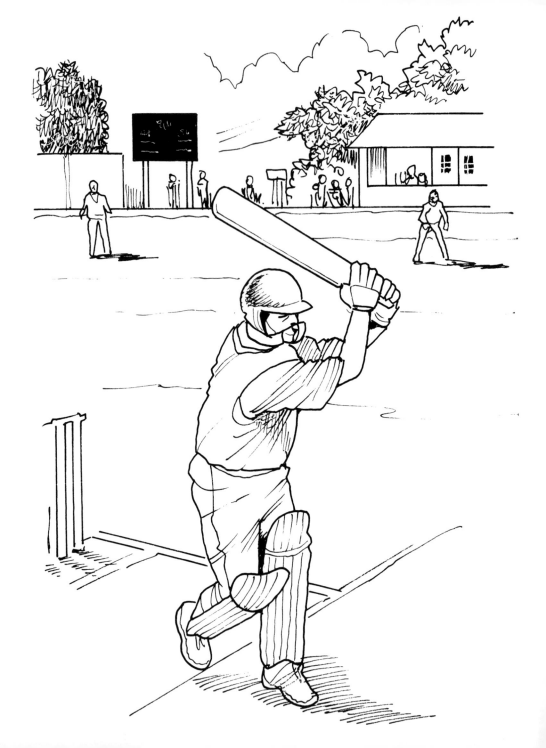

Chapter 2
Batting

EN GARDE!

Before you start your innings, you need to be aware of where the wickets are (alright, I know they're the three sticks that poke up out of the ground!). To aid you in this you first ask the umpire to give you a 'guard'. This is one of the few areas that an umpire may assist a player within the laws of the game. In general, leg stump (sometimes called one leg), middle stump, or middle and leg (sometimes called two legs) are requested.

TAKING YOUR GUARD

This is done by placing the bat on the ground and holding it vertically so that the umpire may clearly guide you to the position which you have requested, then, by scratching this position in the ground with your boot spike, you will know where to place your feet and bat in readiness to face your adversary – the bowler.

KNOW YOUR ENEMY

When you approach the wicket and take your guard always be aware of the fielding positions. It is often possible to ascertain the kind of bowling that you are about to face by observing where the bowler and his captain place their fielders, and in which direction they expect you to hit the ball.

Batting strokes

front-foot
leg-glance

back-foot
defensive

square-cut

sweep

hook

front-foot
off-drive

front-foot
defensive

pull

back-foot
drive

AMBI-WHAT?

Make note, where possible, of the dexterity of the various fielders – are they left- or right-handed or even ambidextrous? This may well hold you in good stead when thinking about whether or not to risk taking a run to them.

GRIPPING STUFF

You must make sure you have the correct grip. If you are a right-handed batsman, the bat is gripped with the left hand above the right, and vice versa should you be a left-handed batsman. Your top hand gives you the control over your strokemaking, whilst your bottom hand predominantly gives you the power behind the shot. Use too much bottom hand and the ball will be hit into the air.

WHERE TO ATTACK

Most of the attacking shots that you will play on the front foot are called 'drives', which project the ball in front of you; the exceptions are the 'sweep' which hits the ball square of the wicket on the 'leg side', and the 'leg glance' which tickles the ball fine behind square on the leg side. The attacking shots which you play on the back foot on the offside are 'cuts' – square cut and the late cut which are directed backward of square of the wicket. Hitting the ball in front of square on the leg side is the 'pull', whilst when you play the ball backward off square on the leg side it's the 'hook'.

The hitting arcs

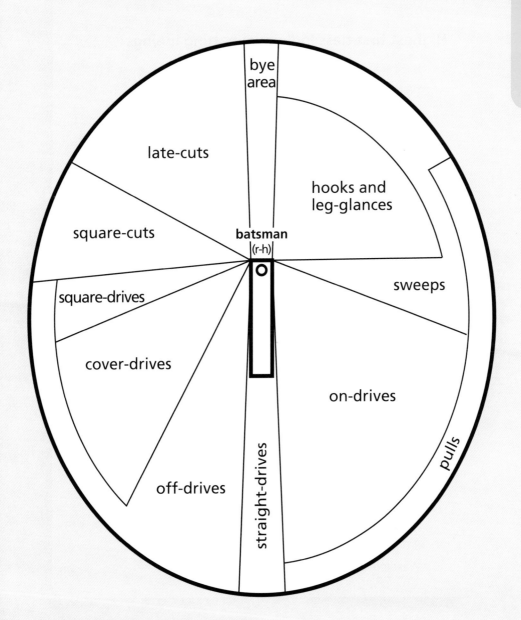

bye
area

late-cuts

hooks and
leg-glances

square-cuts

batsman
(r-h)

sweeps

square-drives

cover-drives

on-drives

off-drives

straight-drives

pulls

Highest first class individual batting innings

1. B C Lara – 501 Not Out
   Warwickshire v Durham. Edgbaston, 1994

2. Hanif Mohammed – 499
   Karachi v Bahawalpur. Karachi, 1958-59

3. D G Bradman – 452 Not Out
   New South Wales v Queensland. Sydney, 1929-30

4. B B Nimbalkar – 443 Not Out
   Maharashtra v Kathiawar. Poona, 1948-49

5. W H Ponsford – 437
   Victoria v Queensland. Melbourne, 1927-28

6. W H Ponsford – 429
   Victoria v Tasmania. Melbourne, 1922-23

7. A Baloch – 428
   Sind v Baluchistan. Karachi, 1973-74

8. A C MacLaren – 424
   Lancashire v Somerset. Taunton, 1895

9. G A Hick – 405 Not Out
   Worcestershire v Somerset. Taunton, 1988

10. B C Lara – 400 Not Out
    West Indies v England. St John's, 2003-04

PLAYING YOUR SHOT

When playing a shot at a full length delivery, it is important to get your front foot close to where the ball pitches, and lean forward to get your head over the bat, thus giving control over your shot.

ON THE BACK FOOT

This is actually where the term originated. A short-pitched delivery, however, is best played with your weight on your back foot, giving you, the batsman, more time to watch the ball, how high it has bounced, and in which direction it is headed.

NUMBER THREE

Should you find yourself batting at number three, then you must be capable of opening the innings too, as on occasions you will be called to the wicket very early on in the innings (as an opening batsmen of many failures I can vouch for this!). You will be called upon to be the backbone of the innings around which the other batsmen will score their runs.

THE MIDDLE ORDER

When you are asked to bat at numbers four to eight, you need to have the capability of consolidating the innings if required, but score rapidly when needed, depending on the state of play. Many a cavalier knock is made in the middle order, and should your top order batsmen have laid solid foundations, you may attack the bowling with gusto – if not brute force!

NINE, TEN, JACK

At nine, ten, and eleven (the tail–enders), although you are not amongst the most gifted of batsmen, you will have two roles. Either to thrash out the final overs to accumulate a large total, or protect your wicket to avoid defeat. (However you can take the glory for either winning or saving a match. If, alas, this is not achieved you can blame the real batsmen for not doing their job properly!)

YOUR MOST IMPORTANT QUALITIES

Your ability to concentrate is crucial to the art of batting. Each ball that the bowler delivers can have a different outcome and must be negotiated on its own merits. It is important to keep your eyes horizontal and maintain a still head. It is harder to pick up the speed and angle of a moving ball if you either tilt or move your head. Remember that at the start of each innings you play, you need time to assess the pace of the wicket, so play yourself in until you are aware of how the pitch is playing before you start playing your attacking shots and building your innings.

TICKING NOT POSING

You should keep looking for single runs; it keeps the scoreboard ticking over and can frustrate the bowlers and fielders alike! Never stand and admire the shot which you have just played, the ball might not reach the boundary and you could miss out on an extra run – plus no-one likes a poser.

ALONG THE GROUND

Unless you are attempting to hit a six, always try to play the ball along the ground – you cannot get caught out that way!

SEEK A PARTNER

Your aim when batting is to score as many runs as possible without getting out. That sounds obvious I know, however, it is often easier to build that run total with the aid of your fellow batsman – your partner. The longer you stay together, the more runs you can accumulate without the bowling side taking another wicket. An innings built with partnerships has more likelihood of achieving a desired total, and thus a victorious conclusion to the game.

Chapter 3
Bowling

TYPES OF BOWLING

There are several kinds of bowling, which can be put into three main categories – fast bowling, medium/swing bowling, and spin bowling. All of these are important in their own way, which one are you? It is best for you to concentrate on specialising on one particular type, don't try to be a Jack of all trades, but master of none!

THE SPEED MERCHANT

As a fast bowler, your armoury is spearheaded by speed. You would expect to be opening the bowling for your side, and use the hardness of the new ball to bounce off the wicket at great pace. The length of your run-up to the wicket is used to produce the pace that you need to deliver the ball, and you can use your bowling action to swing the ball too. The fabled burly fast bowler charging in to bowl at a new batsman, legs and knees pumping like pistons, can be an intimidating sight to a new batsman, and sometimes the wicketkeeper too!

THE MEDIUM PACER

If you are a medium pacer, then you are one of the stock bowlers of club cricket. Your bowling action gives you the ability to swing the ball prodigiously either into or away from the batsmen at varying pace. You will also be more capable of exploiting the conditions of a damp wicket, than other bowlers, by using the seam of the ball to deviate off the surface of the pitch.

WHAT SHOULD YOU AIM FOR?

Whether you are a fast or a medium paced bowler, try to bowl in an imaginary corridor just outside the line of the off stump. (This is well known as Geoffrey Boycott's 'corridor of uncertainty'.) The aim is to commit the batsman into playing a shot at a ball which might deviate off the pitch and take the edge of the bat, giving a catch to the wicketkeeper or the slips, and another scalp to your tally.

THE FEARED BOUNCER

One of the most effective balls that you can bowl as a paceman, is 'the bouncer'. This is pitched short of a length and ideally travels in line with the batsman, putting him on to the back foot and having to fend the ball away from his body. Make sure that you have your close fielders in place for that catch.

OWZEE?

Batsmen often get out when trying to play the ball to an area against the way that it is spinning, resulting in either mis-hitting it into the air or missing the ball completely. (There speaks the voice of experience, believe me!)

THE SPINNERS

No, not the folk group! If you are a spin bowler you must use your art to turn the ball off the wicket. Looking at the wicket from the bowler's end, an 'off break' pitches and turns to the right, whereas a 'leg break' pitches and turns to the left. Not only does a batsman have to read the way in which the ball turns off the wicket, but also has to control the spin on the ball when playing the shot.

FINGER OR WRIST?

Finger-spinners (these tend to be off spinners) use their grip to turn the ball, whereas wrist-spinners (leg spinners), by definition, turn the ball by flexing their wrist at the point of delivery. You have, in your armoury, the ability to disguise the way in which you turn the ball which keeps the batsman on his guard at all times.

RUNNING-UP

Why run-up to the wicket? Well, as a bowler, your run-up to the wicket is as important as the delivery of the ball itself. This gives you the rhythm you need to bowl the ball smoothly; as a fast bowler you can use the momentum of your run-up to give you your pace, as too when you bowl medium pace.

LONG OR SHORT?

If you are bowling spin, you will have a shorter run-up, but your rhythm is just as important for this too.

ACTION MAN

Your bowling action will govern the way that you deliver the ball. For a fast bowler a smooth whippy action after a rhythmic run-up to the wicket can create impressive speed, whereas if you are a swing bowler, you create your art with the way your body is pointing at the delivery stride combined with the way that you hold the ball prior to its release. Conversely as a spin bowler, your grip on the ball and the way in which it is released is all important.

AN IMPORTANT DUTY

At the start of your bowling spell, you must notify the umpire of your 'action', who in turn notifies the batsman. This is confined to whether you, the bowler, bowl with your right arm or your left, and which side of the umpire you will be bowling.

Spinners & cutters

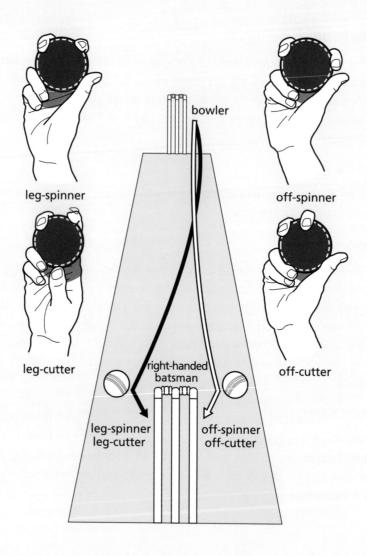

leg-spinner

off-spinner

bowler

leg-cutter

off-cutter

right-handed
batsman

leg-spinner
leg-cutter

off-spinner
off-cutter

Outswingers & inswingers

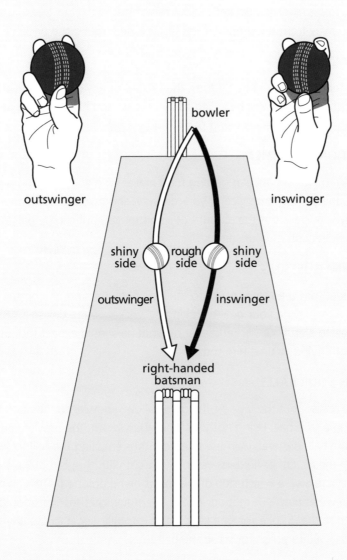

outswinger

inswinger

bowler

shiny side | rough side | shiny side

outswinger | inswinger

right-handed batsman

OVER OR ROUND?

The natural way for you to bowl is with your bowling arm nearest to the umpire, this is 'over the wicket'. Should you bowl with your bowling arm furthest away from the umpire, then this is called 'round the wicket'.

A PENALTY!

Do not forget that you must inform the umpire of any changes to your action otherwise you will be called for a 'no ball' and have to bowl an extra ball in the over, as well as being penalised by a run.

VARIATION ON A THEME

One way to stop a batsman getting too familiar with your bowling is to try a little variety – vary the pace of your delivery, and if you are a spinner, vary not only your pace but the amount of spin that you put on the ball, or even alter the direction of your spin.

KEEP HIM GUESSING

Remember that the more you keep the batsman guessing, the better your chance of achieving your goal by taking his wicket. Try to devise a system of signals to alert your wicketkeeper of what he should expect though – you're not trying to beat him too.

WATCH YOUR BALLS

Did you realise that the laws of the game allow a bowler to maintain the condition of the ball. Using nothing other than sweat, the bowler can polish the ball, preferably on the one side, thus enabling the ball to swing through the air. Other fielders are able to assist with this, but make sure that they are aware which side of the ball is being polished. This can only be done when play is in motion. At the fall of a wicket the ball should be returned to the umpire for safe keeping. It is totally illegal to use any form of artificial aid to polish, or scrub the ball.

Length of deliveries

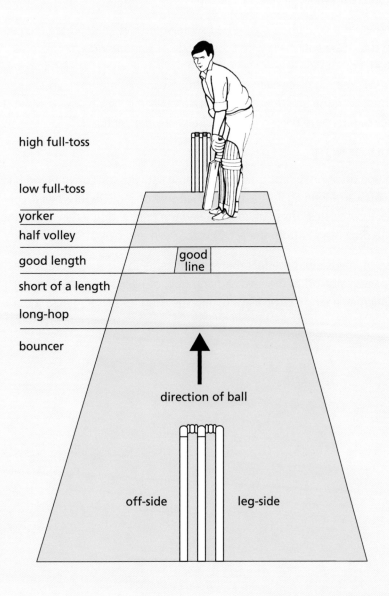

high full-toss

low full-toss

yorker

half volley

good length

good line

short of a length

long-hop

bouncer

direction of ball

off-side

leg-side

A WIND PROBLEM?

It's your own fault for having the bean salad at tea!

If however the weather has turned somewhat more than breezy then you can substitute your bails with those made of Lignum Vitae, sometimes called 'Iron wood'. These are considerably heavier than the standard variety and will keep in place even in fairly strong wind. Please note, you must consult with the umpires on this and normally this only happens when the original bails have been dislodged already by the wind.

BAILS OF NOTE

On one occasion, whilst travelling in Somerset with my co-writer we had a match arranged against a local nomad side of some repute called The Feckless Acolytes. These gentlemen had the unique distinction of playing (with dispensation from the MCC) with green and pink striped bails!

Also of interest was the fact that when it came to the drinks break the Acolytes came on to the field carrying trays of beer and cider! These gentlemen are no longer playing, and speaking for myself, I miss them.

Highest team totals

1. Victoria v New South Wales
   Victoria 1107. Melbourne, 1926-27

2. Victoria v Tasmania
   Victoria 1059. Melbourne, 1922-23

3. Sri Lanka v India
   Sri Lanka 952-6 declared. Colombo, 1997-98

4. Sind v Baluchistan
   Sind 951-7 declared. Karachi, 1973-74

5. Hyderabad v Andhra
   Hyderabad 944-6 declared. Secunderabad, 1993-94

6. New South Wales v South Australia
   New South Wales 918. Sydney, 1900-01

7. Holkar v Mysore
   Holkar 912-8 declared. Indore, 1945-46

8. Railways v Dera Ismail Khan
   Railways 910-6 declared. Lahore, 1964-65

9. England v Australia
   England 903-7 declared. The Oval, 1938

10. Queensland V Victoria
    Queensland 900-6 declared. Brisbane, 2005-06

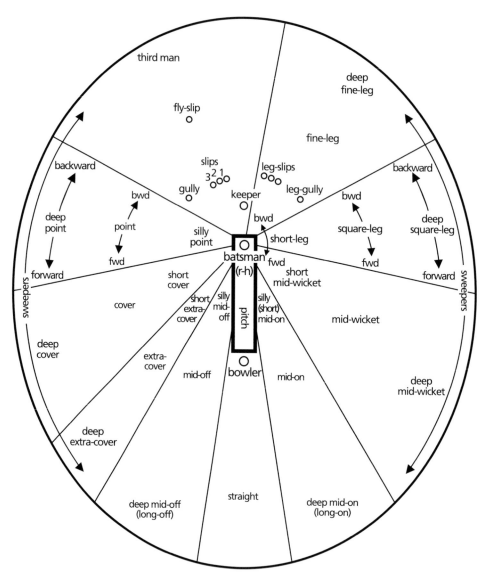

FIELDING POSITIONS

Chapter 4
Fielding

LEGS ON OR OFF?

The field of play is divided into two halves, the leg side and the off side, but how do you decide which is which? Using the wicket as the dividing line, and looking at the batsman's stance, his legs are on the on side or leg side. The other side of the wicket is called the off side. Therefore these alternate between whether a left-handed or right-handed batsman is at the crease.

BE PREPARED

Whichever position you may be fielding, always expect the next ball to come to you. A moment's hesitation or lapse in concentration could cost you a valuable catch and could also mean that you have given away valuable runs to the batting side.

CLOSE FIELDING

Where would you prefer to field? If you choose to be a close fielder, then these are positions predominantly in which to take catches. The slips and gully are situated on the off side within an arc from the wicketkeeper, the closest to him being first slip.

RIGHT ON THE ACTION

The wicketkeeper and first slip are the only fielding positions where, to be successful, the ball is watched from the moment that it leaves the bowler's hand so as to detect any slight deflection from the bat. In all of the other positions, you react from watching the ball off the bat. On the leg side, you could be at leg slip, behind square of the wicket, or at short leg (no, not the player in the side with a height impairment!) where you can be in a catching position forward or backward of square to the wicket.

AROUND THE OUTFIELD

However, moving from slips and gully, you will find 'point' is square to the wicket on the offside. Point can be a catching position or, standing a little deeper, run saving. You then go round to cover, extra cover, and mid-off which is closest to the bowler's wicket. Then moving to the leg, or on, side nearest to the bowler is mid-on moving round to mid-wicket, and square to the batsman's wicket is square leg, and finally you have fine leg. There are variations to the outfield positions. Closer to the batsman is 'silly' as in silly mid-on and in the deep outfield is 'long' (as in long-on).

ON THE MOVE

When you are fielding in the outfield, start to walk towards the batsman as the bowler starts his run-up. By doing so, when the batsman hits the ball you have the momentum to attack the ball and prevent an easy run for the batsman.

KEEP YOUR EYE ON THE BALL

Remember that, having watched the ball leave the bat and come towards you, always watch the ball into your hands before looking where to throw it, otherwise you can fumble or even miss the ball totally. The same goes for catching, watch the ball all the way into your hands.

Chapter 5
Wicketkeeping

GEE 'EM UP

As a focal point, it's up to you to encourage your bowlers and fielders alike – make yourself heard. When the game's not going well, as often happens, you can make the difference between success and failure. Never let your head drop; we can all make mistakes and yours are always high profile because you are the focus of attention. You of all people must forget any mistakes and encourage others with your own performance.

WHERE TO STAND

For the faster bowlers, stand back from the wickets, judging your distance to enable yourself to catch the ball in your midriff. Stand to the offside a little, so that you can observe the bowler's run-up and delivery.

HAVE A CLEAR VIEW

You need to have a clear view of the ball leaving the bowler's hand, and then watch it as it reaches the batsman. Any deflection from the bat that is within your reach is your responsibility. For the spin bowler, and some of the medium pacers, it is better for you to stand up to the wicket. This puts pressure on the batsman, because they can now be stumped, and should prevent them from walking out of their crease to put pressure on your bowlers.

PROTECT YOUR ASSETS

Choose a pair of gloves that are comfortable, they will protect your fingers – your most valuable asset. Wear a pair of chamois or cotton inners, these both absorb your sweat and help absorb the constant impact into your hands of the cricket ball. It is advisable to wear a protective helmet when standing up to the wicket (this is compulsory for anyone aged eighteen and under). Lightweight leg pads do not restrict your movements, and still give you ample protection. And don't forget to wear some form of abdominal guard!

GET TO KNOW YOUR SPIN

Whenever possible, practise with your spin bowlers, and get to know their lines of delivery, the amount that they can turn the ball and the speed at which they bowl. Remember, you will be standing up to them, so you have less reaction time to take the ball when it passes the batsman.

GET THOSE LEGS LOOSE

Practise your leg movements. Moving down the leg side takes a lot of practice and agility is a must. Remember that when you move behind the batsman to take the ball down the leg, for a fraction of a second the batsman blocks your view of the ball and you need to have moved to your position quickly to pre-empt the ball's trajectory into your gloves.

CROUCHING TIGER

Stay in your crouched stance as long as possible and move up from the ground with the ball, so that you take the ball in your gloves with an upward movement. It is much harder for you to take the ball cleanly with a downward movement – and easier to drop it!

SECRET CODES

Discuss signals with your bowlers for any surprise deliveries they might want to use to beat a batsman; it gives the bowler more confidence and can be a useful addition to his armoury and, of course, yours.

TALK THEM OUT

As the nearest person to the batsman, make yourself heard, let him know you are there to pounce on his mistakes. Don't 'sledge' him, but try to engage him in conversation, ask about his wife or girlfriend, what he's doing after the match – it can break his concentration!

GOT HIM!

I recall a batsman having reached a faultless half-century, when a very attractive young lady appeared on the pavilion steps apparently waving at him. Between deliveries, I asked who it was – 'my new girlfriend' came the very proud reply, and he was able to spend the rest of the innings with her in the pavilion because he was bowled out next ball!

Chapter 6
Captaincy

RIGOURS OF THE JOB

As a captain you must not only be a good tactician on the field of play, but an ambassador for your club, a man manager, an organiser, a selector, a nursemaid, an agony aunt, but most importantly you must have broad shoulders and a thick skin, because you won't be able to please everyone all the time! You must be able to contact your team at any given time to check availability, to inform players of their selection or, just as importantly, non-selection!

READING THE SIGNS

It is essential for you to have a good knowledge of the game, know the attributes of your own team, and have the ability to pick out weaknesses in the opposition. This can give you, as a captain, the advantage. When winning the toss you should be able to read the wicket and know whether to bat first if the conditions are preferable, or put the opposing team in to bat if you think that your bowlers are able to make good use of the wicket and bowl them out.

HAVE NO FEAR

You must use diplomatic guile to establish your authority over your team. And you must be confident in the decisions that you make, however controversial, and if necessary discuss your actions to explain, for instance, why a particular bowler has been changed, or why you have rearranged the batting order or placed the field in a certain way.

YOU DO HAVE AN ALLY!

Don't fret because you are not totally on your own. One of your duties is to appoint a lieutenant, a confidante – yes a Vice Captain. (I love that name.) He can take on some of those off-the-field burdens for you. Such as taking next week's availabilities, collecting the match fees, paying the tea ladies, and organising other jobs amongst your team. He is also there for consultation of tactics and team selection.

AFTER HOSTILITIES

Remember that you are also an ambassador, and as such there are niceties to attend to after the game has finished. Thank the officials – umpires and scorers alike remember your appreciation which can stand you in good stead in the future. Once in the bar buy your opposite number a drink, and of course do not forget to thank the tea ladies!

MAINTAIN LINES OF COMMUNICATION

You must make yourself clear and understood by all. Likewise you need to understand others too. Lack of communication can prove very embarrassing. I recall meeting at the club for an away game, making sure all of my troops had transport. One of my team had a very expensive car, and departing with his passenger – my opening batsman – he shouted that his kit was in the Porsche. Once we had all arrived some thirty minutes later my opener gave me a puzzled look and asked where his kit was. He had left it in the PORCH of the cricket club. Needless to say I retrieved it in double quick time and arrived back within minutes of the game's start time.

So in summary, if you are the captain you must:

- Use authority wisely.

- Trust your vice captain.

- Keep discipline on the field.

- Thank the officials after the game.

- Share a beer afterwards with the opposition.

- Not forget to thank the tea ladies!

Chapter 7

Equipment

KEEPING IT ALL TOGETHER

You will need a large receptacle in which to keep all of your kit. Cricket bags come in various shapes and sizes, from the hard sided 'coffin' to the larger hold-all type complete with wheels on the bottom. Believe me, when you have packed all the kit that you might need for a cricket match, these can be invaluable.

BATMAN

Cricket bats are traditionally crafted from English willow, and are available in different sizes and weights. This is just as well, because so are the players. Some players make the mistake of thinking the heavier the bat the better and the farther it will hit the ball, believe me I can personally attest that this is not the case.

GETTING IT READY

When purchasing a new cricket bat, make sure that you know how to make it ready for use. Some bats need oiling with linseed before use and then knocked-in with a bat mallet to harden the playing surface of the blade (and the edges). Others come with a protective surface on the face of the bat but still require knocking in. You can also buy bats that are ready to go.

GET A GRIP

A bat that feels the right weight, grip, and balance is to be more sought after. It's always best to shop around and get the right feel for you. There are different kinds of rubber grips (a sleeve that fits over the bat handle) and they need to be replaced if worn or torn.

KEEP A GRIP

I remember batting in a 20-over match using an old and trusted bat with a worn rubber grip, having a huge pull to square leg (as I often do), the bat slipping out of my hands, scoring four runs, but almost decapitating the umpire at square leg with my bat at the same time! Sometimes it is comfortable to use two or even three grips on the same handle.

HANDLE IT WELL

The vast majority of bats have round handles, however some manufacturers' bats have oval handles. Paul Bradbury, for instance, a well-known Australian bat maker and good friend to Roly and me, produces oval handles on his bats, and they are my personal choice as I find them easier to grip.

THE GLOVES

Protecting your hands when batting is imperative, and to do this there are specially designed batting gloves. It is also advisable for you to wear a pair of thin cotton inners to absorb sweat. But take note there are differences between pairs of gloves for right – and left-handed batsmen – beware when purchasing. Remember, they are great for cricket but not much use for playing the piano.

PAD UP

Make sure you choose the ones that are right for you. Try them on in the shop. There are several designs of batting pads, varying in padding, weights and of course, as with the batting gloves, there are differences between left-handed and right-handed pads. If you are a wicketkeeper, you can choose lightweight pads that are cut off just above the knee. If you intend to go in for shin guards, these are recommended for close in fielding positions.

TAKING IT ON THE CHIN

If you are over eighteen it is advisable to wear a protective helmet when batting. (It is mandatory that all batsmen under the age of 18 wear helmets, whilst playing or practising!) You can also wear a helmet when you are keeping wicket, or fielding close to the batsman.

SO TO THE FEET

Are you a batsman or a bowler? There are boots available designed for bowlers and batsmen alike. Cricket boots traditionally have spikes on the heel and sole, however there are boots available with rubber heels and spikes on the sole only. I would always advise spikes in wet conditions. It's very common to see a player slip in the wet if not wearing spikes.

INSURANCE FOR THE JEWELS!

This is a must for you, whether batsman, wicketkeeper, or a close fielder you need to wear abdominal protection – known as a 'box'. These are slotted into pouches in jockstraps or cricketers' jockey pants, some of which have pockets for inner thigh guards too.

WHAT ABOUT A THIGH PAD?

Have you ever been hit on the fleshy part of the thigh by a cricket ball when you have been batting? I can assure you that it is quite painful so it is advisable to wear a thigh pad on your front leg when batting. These are strapped to your thigh beneath your whites (trousers) and protect the area above your batting pads.

TO CAP IT ALL

If you are playing for a team on a regular basis, lash out and buy a cap. These are not only decorative, but also very useful especially to keep the sun off your head in warm weather. Unfortunately, the trend nowadays is for the baseball type, although you can still get both the traditional and Aussie baggie styles. Remember you can, if you're lucky, be at the wicket for some time. Like your sweater your cap should be in your club colours.

As a summary then, you will need:

- A bat – choose wisely!

- A pair of pads – make sure they are a good fit.

- Whites – including shirts and trousers.

- Sweater – either long or short sleeve.

- Batting gloves (don't forget your liners).

- Jock strap (or box) and support.

- Boots – try different styles.

- Socks (of course!).

- A cap – preferably in club colours.

- A bag or coffin to put it all in.

Chapter 8
Practice

MAKES PERFECT?

During the close season, practice sessions are held indoors, these are normally called 'nets' and you would do well to attend. There are many schools nowadays with indoor sports facilities available, many of these offer cricket netting facilities. Most county cricket clubs offer specialised netting with the option of coaching.

KEEPING YOUR HAND IN

Netting keeps you acclimatised to using your hand to eye co-ordination. It keeps those muscles in tune that you wouldn't otherwise be using and keeps you in touch with your other cricketing colleagues. I heartily advise nets. Another sport which is excellent for hand to eye co-ordination is table-tennis, but don't forget to use a proper ball – cricket balls don't bounce very well and ruin the table!

TAKING IT SERIOUSLY

Whether indoors or outdoors, bowling and batting techniques should be enhanced during net sessions. As a batsman or bowler you should use this facility seriously for practising and developing skills, ironing out any problems with technique and assisting team mates with their problems too.

MECHANICAL CRICKET

Some clubs will also have the facility of a bowling machine, which can be set to project a ball at a certain area of the wicket, and it can also be set at different speeds; this can be used to strengthen a batsman's weaker shots.

IT'S AN EYE THING

You should always try to keep your eyes attuned to the ball. Fielding and catching is an area of the game in which practice is often disregarded, and yet it is an essential part of cricket. Some clubs have a catching net, a net within a metal frame at which the ball is thrown and the rebound is caught.

THE CRADLE

Another piece of equipment is a 'slip cradle', this is made of several curved slats of wood secured to a frame and placed horizontally on the ground. When a ball is thrown at it from one end, it is deflected at an angle off the curved slats at the opposite end to resemble an edged ball off a cricket bat. A simple alternative is throwing a tennis ball at a wall and catching the rebound.

THE PRE-MATCH WARM UP

I must recommend this to you as part of your regime prior to playing. Before a game, it is essential that players do warm up exercises to avoid pulling muscles during the game, and after the game finishes, warm down exercises, thus reducing the possibility of muscular damage. This is especially important in this country, with the temperatures in which we start and end the cricket season!

STRETCHING IT A BIT

Try stretching exercises to start off with; they will help loosen you up. A simple arms over the head will do first and then move on to stretching your arms down by your legs. After each exercise, though, just give yourself a shake to loosen any tightness before you attempt the next one. You will probably have to reach hard and even perhaps dive for a good catch. The field will not be impressed if you suddenly lock into position and have to be helped off the pitch.

KEEP IT QUICK

You do not have to spend too long on a warm up. After all you don't want to be knackered before you start; 15 minutes is ample. But you can keep yourself loose throughout the game, doing simple, short exercises in between overs or in breaks of play.

SURPRISE ME

Try standing as a team in a large circle and throwing the ball to each other as quickly as possible and without warning. This keeps your reactions sharp. But don't get too zealous – you don't want to break any fingers!

KEEP EVERYONE BUSY

Get the wicketkeeper to put on his gloves, and stand by a stump in the ground. He will throw the ball to a player by him with a cricket bat, who in turn hits the ball either in the air for a catch or along the ground toward a ring of fielders some 30 yards away. The fielder in turn catches, or gathers the ball off the ground and returns the ball to the keeper just above the stump as quickly as possible, who then repeats the procedure.

PRACTISING ON THE SQUARE

Ask your groundsman (nicely) to prepare a wicket on the perimeter of your square for match practice. This will enable both your batsmen and your bowlers to assimilate match conditions, more so than using the artificial surfaces of the fixed net practice areas outside the boundary.

KEEP IT REGULAR

Designate a mutually convenient night of the week for your practice sessions, you want as many of your players to attend as possible. Try to vary the routine, changing the emphasis from fielding to catching to batting to bowling – do not let players stagnate.

CATCH THE COACH

Your club may well have a qualified cricket coach. Indeed if you have a junior section, it will be a certainty. Ask him or her to advise you about whichever part of your game needs to be resolved.

JUST TO SUMMARISE:

- Take practice seriously.

- Warm up first.

- Practise slip catches (with a cradle if possible).

- Use stretching exercises.

- Don't overdo it.

- Involve everyone.

> " I tend to think that cricket is the greatest thing that God ever created on earth – certainly greater than sex, although sex isn't too bad either. "

Ian Botham

Part Two
Groundmanship

Chapter 1
Tools of the Trade

YOUR BASIC HAND TOOLS

To maintain a cricket square and outfield requires much specialised equipment, however basic needs can be covered with the use of standard items such as a bass broom, a besom or witch's brush, shovel, watering can, paint pot, 1" (2.5 cm) paint brush, wheelbarrow, hosepipe long enough to reach the square from your water tap, 30yds (27 m) of strong twine, a minimum 30yd (27 m) measuring tape, and the old faithful garden rake. Don't forget, all groundsmen are expected to work in extreme weather conditions, so a good pair of waterproofs and Wellington boots are essential. Don't forget all garages or huts need a well-stocked first-aid kit in case of mishaps.

MAKING YOUR MARK

Each wicket has to be marked out with white lines. These are drawn using a custom made wooden or metallic frame. A stump marker is used to make holes at the correct spacing and depth for the stumps to be easily set out before a game.

AFTER MATCH WORK

To repair used wickets prior to reseeding, use a spiker. A levelling frame such as a trulute is used for spreading loam and soil evenly over small repaired areas; for spreading evenly over larger areas, you will need a drag-mat. A back-pack pressurised sprayer is used for spreading various liquid feeds to the square throughout the season; and then to water the square evenly, you will need a sprinkler system to attach to your hosepipe.

TOYS FOR THE BOYS

Ideal requirements are two petrol-driven cylinder mowers, the first a minimum 24" (60 cm) blade on a low cut setting for cutting the wicket, the second a minimum 30" (76 cm) blade set to a higher cut for the rest of the playing area (the square).

ON A ROLL

Once again you require two rollers, the lighter can be either hand–drawn or mechanical. This is used for lightly rolling the wicket in between innings on the match day itself, and a heavy mechanical roller 1 to 1.5 ton (similar to a tarmacadam roller), but never use on 'vibrate' setting; this may well put a smile on the driver's face but will kill off the grass! In the good old days, horses were used to draw such rollers, presumably also providing a good source of fertiliser!

MAKE A CUT ON THE OUTFIELD

There are two choices here, either a set of gang-mowers pulled by a tractor, or sit-on mowers (such as Ransomes) which can give a closer cut.

FINAL TOUCHES

Don't forget we groundsmen are responsible for the areas outside of the playing area too. So a rotary mower for rough grass and a petrol strimmer are needed to keep on top of the undergrowth.

SOAKING UP THE PRESSURE

Although considered a luxury, it is necessary to have some form of equipment to soak up excess surface water on match days, such as a Sopper or Bowdry. Although I have experienced the use of large slabs of foam to soak up the water, then squeezed out through an old-fashioned washing mangle on the perimeter of the field!

ESSENTIAL MAINTENANCE

During the close season, put your mowers in for servicing and repair, and have your roller serviced and put under cover. Your equipment is vital, and keeping it maintained will prolong its life and efficiency.

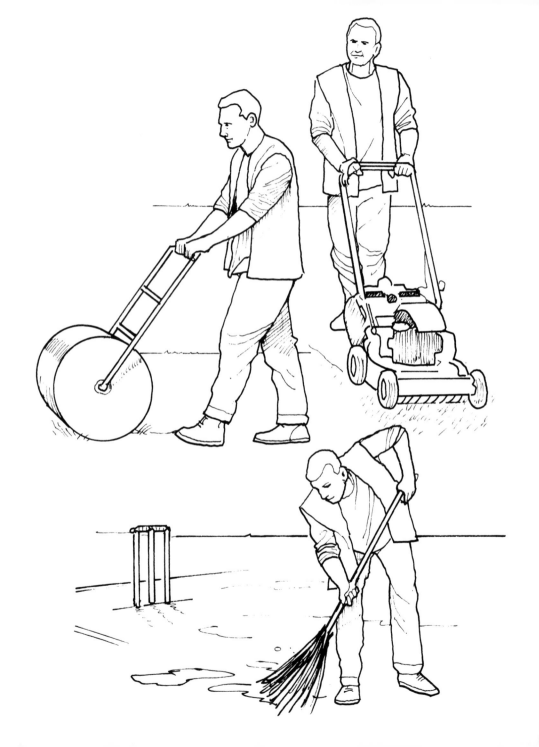

Chapter 2
Grounds Treatment

PRE-SEASON

KEEP IN TRIM

Having kept an eye on your precious piece of land over the winter, and maintained a cut to an even height (approx. 1"), when the milder and drier weather permits (around mid to late March) work can commence in earnest.

BRUSHING AND ROLLING

Before the first light roll, use your besom to disperse any wormcasts, which will minimise muddy blotches that could discourage grass growth. From this point onwards until the end of the season it is advisable to brush the square whenever possible to displace the moisture off the leaves of the grass. Disease can enter the leaves from the moisture droplets so dispersal to the soil helps to defend against such problems.

IRONING OUT

Provided the square is not too wet, use your lightest roller and cover the whole square initially left to right (square of the wickets), then diagonally, and finally in line with the wickets, thus ironing out any creasing. Think of rolling out pastry, and spreading it to make a nice even base – it's a similar procedure but on a much larger scale! After repeating this procedure, and providing the ground is not too wet, you can then progress to do the same with your medium weighted roller.

DON'T LOSE YOUR ROOTS

Remember that the ground is still soft and to use too heavy a roller at this stage will break the roots of the new grass, and cause ridges to form. By rolling in this way, you are consolidating the square, and slowly building the depth of compaction evenly, thus achieving the aim of a wicket with pace and evenness of bounce. Finally, once weather allows, progress to your heavy roller.

END OF SEASON

THINNING OUT

This is the time of renovation. Firstly, cut the whole square down to the height of a match day wicket. The square must be thoroughly scarified to remove all dead grass (thatch) to encourage growth for new grass seed. This is done several times until you are satisfied that all thatch has been removed from the surface of the square, each time changing direction by a few degrees.

TOP DRESSER

The next step is spiking. Using a solid tiner, spike the whole square, this aerates the ground and makes holes for the seed to bed into. The seed is spread evenly over the square, and then an autumn fertiliser can be applied. Finally the top dressing is applied and evenly spread, this is a cricket loam, a special 25% clay based soil, giving an ideal firm surface for playing cricket in England.

BUT MY CLUB HASN'T GOT THIS EQUIPMENT!

Scarifiers, tiners, and top dressing spreading equipment is all available for hire, as not many cricket clubs have the funding to purchase these specialised machines. There are companies that offer these services and are able to advise on treatments – I have been indebted to the help from my good friend Dave Bates of Earthtec for his advice and help in my work at Hammerwich C.C. Alternatively, good relations with a neighbouring cricket club could result in a sharing of necessary equipment and splitting the cost of servicing and repairs.

DON'T FORGET THE REST

The end of the season is also time to batten down the hatches for the other equipment such as site-screens. These should be sheltered away from the seasonal high winds and checked for any pre-season maintenance that might be required. Check the score-box too for similar signs of wear and tear.

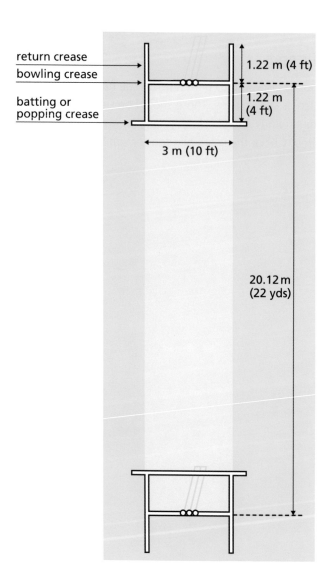

return crease

bowling crease

batting or
popping crease

1.22 m (4 ft)

1.22 m
(4 ft)

3 m (10 ft)

20.12 m
(22 yds)

TRACK MARKING AND DIMENSIONS

Chapter 3
The Wicket & the Square

USE YOUR MATHS

You need to mark out the wickets for the season before you can prepare them. By using Pythagorus' theorem ('the square of the hypotenuse of a right–angled triangle is equal to the sum of the squares of the other two sides') otherwise known as the 3:4:5 method of triangulation, you can ensure that the playing square IS square.

STAY AHEAD OF THE PLOT

Planning is essential for wicket preparation. At any one time, you should have two to three wickets at various stages of readiness. However they must never be adjacent to one another, as this risks damage to your preparations. Work should start at least a week prior to play. Roll with the heavy roller at as slow a pace as possible for around 30 minutes. Brush the wicket prior to cutting, and then cut in the opposite direction dropping the mower to a low setting. This treatment is done on a daily basis until the day of the match itself. The ideal time of the day to roll the wicket is as early in the morning as possible. This allows the heat of the day to evaporate the moisture, which has been squeezed to the surface by your slow rolling.

FINAL PREPARATIONS

On the day of the match, using the pitch marker, paint the lines to a maximum of 1" (2.5 cm) width, make the holes for the stumps with the stump-marker, and fill the holes with water, this helps putting the stumps into the ground and can also prevent them snapping at the base when your fast bowler hits the wickets! If there is any chance of inclement weather, ensure that there is sawdust available for the bowlers' footmarks.

IT'S YOUR CALL

Remember a well-prepared wicket will probably reach its peak during its third or fourth day of play, provided the ends are maintained, so do not bow to pressure if the 1st team captain insists on a new wicket for each of his home games!

ONGOING REPAIRS

During the match, between innings, the bowlers' creases and the batting creases may need to be swept and repainted before the start of the second innings.

WHAT IS THE SQUARE?

The square is the area comprising all your playing wickets. A square is 22 yds (20.12 m) in length and the width is determined by the number of wickets you require. A wicket is 10 ft (3m) wide, so a square such as mine at Hammerwich C.C. with 14 wickets on it, is 22 yds (20.12 m) by 140 ft (42 m).

BE VIGILANT

Having done your initial pre-season rolling, and squared it off, your surface should be level and hardened off. Keep an eye out for any discolouration or weed growth. Growth enhancers can be sprayed on the square with the correct advice and in the right conditions using your back-pack equipment.

GIVE IT A DRINK

Water your square at the end of the day, when there is less chance of the water evaporating, thus allowing more to soak in and nourish the grass roots and seedlings to your repaired ends.

WATCH OUT FOR THE LURGY!

Depending on the rate of growth of the grass keep it cut to a height of
½", keeping an eye out for any diseased areas and repairing any damaged
areas.

REAP THE PRAISE

When possible, monitor the root growth in several areas of the square.
The deeper your root growth – the stronger your grass will be; the stronger
your grass – the better the performance of the wickets that you will play
on in terms of pace and bounce; and of course the better the pace and
bounce – the more praise you will get from the people who are playing
on it!

Chapter 4
Outfield and Ongoing Maintenance

ROLLING AGAIN

Frosts can lift the ground surface during the winter, so level the ground during the milder, wet period around mid-March using a tractor-pulled roller or, at a push, use your heavy roller even though this might be an arduous and time-consuming task.

KEEP IT FAST

To maintain a quick outfield, the grass on it should be cut at least once a week. Do not let your outfield grow too long as, when it is cut, the long grass cuttings will slow down the ball during the match.

MORE REPAIR WORK

You can guarantee that bowlers with long run-ups will gouge lines in your outfield with their spiked boots rather than use the bowlers' markers that the umpires will have provided. Mix a little loam and soil with some seed, wet the area, spike it then dress with your soil and seed mixture, and re-water. Observe any areas that need weed treatment or reseeding at the end of the season, and add to your end of season work. Keep a check on your net practice areas, and maintain as per the wicket preparation. The practice surface should be near match condition.

All ten wickets in an innings (post 1945)

1. W E Hollies
   Warwickshire v Nottinghamshire. Birmingham, 1946

2. J M Simms
   East v West. Kingston upon Thames, 1948

3. J K R Graveney
   Gloucestershire v Derbyshire. Chesterfield, 1949

4. T E Bailey
   Essex v Lancashire. Clacton, 1949

5. R Berry
   Lancashire v Worcestershire. Blackpool, 1953

6. S P Gupte
   President's XI v Combined XI. Bombay, 1954-55

7. J C Laker
   Surrey v Australians. The Oval, 1956

8. K Smales
   Nottinghamshire v Gloucestershire. Stroud, 1956

9. G A R Lock
   Surrey v Kent. Blackheath, 1956

10. J C Laker
    England v Australia. Manchester, 1956

BE A DIPLOMAT AS WELL

It is always advisable to be diplomatic when tending to the ground perimeters. If any course of action needs to be taken in cutting back trees and undergrowth, check with the local environment or wildlife organisations for advice. Apart from enhancing the local wildlife habitat, it keeps your club in the good books with the local community.

SECURITY DOGS

Local dog walkers can be the bain of a groundsman's life, but if approached, most are understanding of our problems and will assist in cleaning up their mess. If you can keep them to the perimeter of your playing area, they will cause few problems, and in a community can also be good security, by keeping an eye on your outbuildings and machinery.

WET AND DRY

English summers can be very fickle, and being one step ahead of the weather is a groundsman's trait. Find out the best local forecasts. Cover your wicket with appropriate sheeting or wheel-on covers, and don't forget those areas of the square that might get slippery in the wet, such as bare ends of old wickets or repaired and freshly loamed areas.

BE PREPARED

Keep a good supply of sawdust for the bowlers' and batsmen's footmarks, but remember to clean this up after the game, as sawdust does not encourage grass growth. Saved sweepings from used wickets can also be used in certain areas to soak up moisture, sometimes mixed with grass cuttings. It is advisable to maintain a wicket at the extremity of the square for use in wet weather. This will give an alternative wicket to play on and apply damage limitation to the rest of the square and the prepared wickets.

NO BLACK MARKS PLEASE

If you start to roll your wicket with your heavy roller, and the wicket goes black – stop what you are doing because it's too wet; come back when the water has dissipated further.

CLEANING UP

After a match, wickets must be swept and all debris swept up. This can be kept and mixed with loam to cover newly-laid seed, or used in wet areas on damp days. Shave the wicket with your mower and roll very slowly to flatten any new divots on the playing area. When a wicket has been used for the last time, wet the bare areas, spike, spread seed, then cover with loam and soil mixture, spreading out evenly with your trulute, and then water.

SET THE PACE

Fast bowlers tend to cause most damage with their front footmarks. These can be repaired with a mixture of loam and cement. Wet the area first, make your wet mix and fill the holes, smooth over and allow to set. This will enable you to get another match from a good wicket. I would suggest a few testers first to get the mix right, the bowlers do not want to land on a slab of concrete, likewise too soft a mix will be dug out within the first over.

GIVE YOUR SQUARE THE ONCE-OVER

After each match, check over the whole square, looking for gouges or divots created by fielders during the match. These can be raised by using a small hand fork, and then rolled to give an even surface.

THERE'S ALWAYS HELP AT HAND

Don't ever be afraid or too proud to ask for help if you have a problem with your ground. Each county will have a Groundsman Association which will be able to advise you if you cannot find a more local solution. Here in England I often go to STAG do's (no, not that kind – STaffordshire Association of Groundsmen!). Remember that we groundsmen are not loners – you won't be the first to have had a problem and it's good to talk! Try talking to other local club groundsmen, they may have experienced the same problem as you, or may be able to lend/hire you the equipment that you might require. If none of the above can help try the Institute of Groundsmanship website – **www.iog.org**.

" Cricket gives one a chance to play the man and act gentleman. *"*

Sir Frederick Toone

Part Three
Umpiring

Chapter 1
Umpire's Clothing and Equipment

If you are already an experienced umpire you will know the importance of 'creating the right image' when on the field of play. An umpire is a figure of authority and should dress accordingly.

It is essential for the umpire to be recognisable at a glance. Remember this is not achieved by multicoloured, knee length shorts or indeed any other dubious apparel.

THE WHITE COAT

The adopting of the white coat is quite sufficient to lend dignity to the occasion. I personally deplore the donning of the 'pastel' shades now seen in 20/20 matches and 'pyjama' cricket games. They are reminiscent of ice cream salesmen or second rate dentists.

There are a number of different styles of white umpire's coats available to choose from. At one time the longer 'lab coat" was in vogue and, indeed, that is the style I prefer but nowadays it's more normal for umpires to adopt the shorter length of coat.

THE CLOTHES HORSE

For maximum effect this should be equipped with side straps which fasten to the hip area of the coat. This is in order that the Umpire may accommodate the sweater of the player who is bowling at his end. The sweater is easily held in this way while the Bowler performs his office.

THE DEADLY 'FLY-AWAY'

The Umpire may also be requested to take the Bowler's cap or hat whilst the player is bowling during that over. This is for the very best of reasons. If a bowler were to commence his run up or delivery while wearing head gear of some sort it may become dislodged from his head and fall to the pitch and either become entangled in the bowler's feet or obstruct the delivery in some other way.

In addition to this, a hat or cap might, conceivably, fall and dislodge the bails from their position on the stumps and in so doing render that delivery as a 'Dead Ball' until the bails are replaced in order that the over may continue.

Apart from these occasions it is always best to keep in mind that the Umpire is there to ensure fair play and not to be treated as a convenient hat stand or clothing repository.

GET AHEAD, GET A HAT

The Umpire may, of course, wear head apparel himself. Indeed, particularly on sunny days it is advisable. The best, in my view, are those that follow the general design now generically termed as the 'Panama'. This is the plain cream straw hat of a trilby variety and may be adorned with a club or association coloured hatband; very smart and very useful.

Also club caps may be worn, although the Umpire should be seen as having no particular club affinity as he is, or should be, an impartial officer to the game.

During friendly games the rulings may be relaxed and, indeed, I have been known to stand wearing an old 'Arab Legion' head-dress, this has caused some mirth on occasion and once caused me to be 'fined' during a charity match, as the bright colours were said to have put off the bowlers!

THE OCULAR DISCUSSION

The subject of using sunglasses has, on occasion, caused discussion among some of my fellow umpires and scorers. It is best to remember that a few years ago a lot of sunglasses available could dim the sight as well as the glare, but now happily there are many makes that do not cause any distortion at all.

The Umpire's vision is his most powerful tool. Anything that inhibits his sight should be avoided.

How well I remember one particular old friend of mine whom I had not seen for some years. He duly turned up for a match clad in the white coat and I asked him how long he had been umpiring. I remembered him as a fine fast bowler. 'Only for a couple of years' he said, 'Ever since my eyes started to go'! I had to smile, I knew exactly what he meant but what an unfortunate choice of terminology in which to express his reasoning.

Wicketkeeping:
Eight dismissals (or more) in an innings

1. Tahir Rashid – 9 wkts
   Habib Bank v PACO. Gujranwala, 1992-93

2. W R James – 9 wkts
   Matabeleland v Mashonaland CD. Bulawayo, 1995-96

3. A T W Grout – 8 wkts
   Queensland v Western Australia. Brisbane, 1959-60

4. D E East – 8 wkts
   Essex v Somerset. Taunton, 1985

5. S A Marsh – 8 wkts
   Kent v Middlesex. Lords, 1991

6. T J Zoehrer – 8 wkts
   Australians v Surrey. The Oval, 1993

7. D S Berry – 8 wkts
   Victoria v South Australia. Melbourne, 1996-97

8. Y S S Mendis – 8 wkts
   Bloomfield v Kurunegala Youth. Colombo, 2001-02

9. S Nath – 8 wkts
   Assam v Tripura. Gauhati, 2001-02 (on his debut)

10. J N Batty – 8 wkts
    Surrey v Kent. The Oval, 2004

THE SCRIBE

The Umpire should also carry a small pad and pencil, this enables him to jot down any occurrences as well as to keep track of the overs and score although this should be clearly shown on the scoreboard. At times the Umpire may notice a discrepancy on the board and therefore may need to inform the Scorers of the same, after all, everyone is human but then again so are umpires.

BALLS!

It is also necessary for the Umpire to carry something with which to count the number of balls that are being delivered in each over. This may be a simple matter of having six small pebbles in his pocket and transferring one to his other hand as each ball is bowled, however, there are also some devices that can be purchased for the more serious umpire. These are very reasonably priced and normally adopt the form of a 'Clicker' which registers the balls as the finger depresses or releases on the counter.

I personally have long favoured a holder that contains six pound coins, which can be released easily and replaced easily too between overs. It also gives the Umpire the appearance of being somewhat affluent, not a bad thing when inspiring confidence in others.

DAMP, A SOLUTION

In addition to these items the Umpire should also carry a small towel of the 'Beer' variety. This is absolutely vital if the weather is turning damp, an altogether too common an occurrence in Britain I'm afraid.

This small towel is used to wipe the ball when handed to the Bowler in between deliveries. A wet or muddy ball is not permissable for accurate or fair delivery when being bowled.

BAILS

Spare bails should also be carried by the Umpire. In fact he should go as far to as to have his own and keep them to hand for every match at which he officiates. Bails can be easily lost or damaged.

In the event of heavy winds it is also necessary for the Umpire to go out to the wicket carrying a special set of heavier bails which are readily available at most sports stores. Heavy winds can easily dislodge a normal weight bail and thus render it necessary to replace the lighter weight with those of a more robust nature, being made from heavier wood.

Please note that if this happens during the match the Scorers should be informed in order that they can record it in the score book.

MORE BALLS

One of the most important items that should be carried is, needless to say, a spare ball. This should not be new but of good used quality. The Umpire will inspect the balls to be used as spares before he allows them to be bowled. In point of fact, most colleagues of mine carry up to two spares as it is an all too frequent a sight to see a ball being hit and 'lost' in the grounds surrounding smaller clubs and having a replacement ensures minimum disruption to the proceedings.

TEMPUS FUGIT

A good watch or timepiece is also of great importance. This is vital for the timing of play and any interruptions that may take place. The watches of the Umpire and the Scorer should be compared before the start of each match. The choice should then be made whose watch will be used as the official timekeeper.

THE MARKER

Very often the home ground of the club that is playing at Home will supply a bowlers' start marker. This is often just a simple round piece of metal or plastic that is commonly white in colour and used by the Bowler to mark the start of his run up. It is a good idea for the Umpire to carry one of these as well. You never can tell when it can come in handy.

Let's recap the average kit needs for an umpire:

- A white coat.

- Some kind of hat if necessary.

- Sunglasses if the weather is bright.

- At least one spare ball.

- A set of bails.

- Something to count the balls in the over with (pebbles, coins etc).

- A small towel.

- A small pad and pencil or pen.

- A Bowlers' start marker.

Chapter 2
Umpire's Conduct

An Umpire must lend an air of dignity to the game and not be intrusive to the proceedings. Nothing is worse than an officiating Umpire being deliberately confrontational.

When standing as an Umpire you may (all too frequently in today's modern games) become the target for forms of abuse from players on the field. Remember, the laws of the game are on your side. Never reciprocate with like behaviour, rise above it and take action at a later time in the game by speaking to the Captains.

THE ALL IMPORTANT DECISION

It must be recognized that the decision given by the Umpire during the course of a game is final. On occasion those who are playing or spectating may disagree, the Umpire's decision stands.

The Umpire is not required to explain his decisions to those who question him, indeed, it is advisable not to. This could lead to confrontation and a disruption in the game. If absolutely necessary the Umpire may speak quietly with the questioning player after the game, even referring to the official MCC book of laws if required to.

Those who are viewing a game of cricket, some perhaps for the first time, must be able to have confidence in the Umpire's actions and decisions. With this in mind the Umpire must be confident in his own actions.

REMEMBER, THOU ART BUT HUMAN

Please remember, all men make mistakes and the Umpire is not an exception. We can only try to ensure that mistakes are kept to a bare minimum and this is best done by studying the laws of the game and putting them into practice to the best of our ability.

One of the most important rulings that an Umpire must remember is that if there is ever any doubt at all when an appeal has been made in order to dismiss a Batsman that the doubt must go in favour of the Batsman, at all times.

THE MENACE OF TELEVISION

In these times of television replays it is sometimes clear by our viewing that on occasion an Umpire has made a mistake in judgement, it is easy for us to see in slow motion and viewed repeatedly on our screens but the Umpire sees it just once and at speed. He, or she let us remember, has to make that decision in a literal split second and that decision must stand.

VERBIAGE

There are times when 'standing' during a match that the Umpires may hear verbiage being delivered by players in order to unbalance the opposition. This has become known as 'Sledging'; it is a deplorable activity and I for one am continually saddened by its continued use and apparent growth.

Whereas there is no law that prohibits this vile behaviour the Umpire may and should intervene if in his judgement the actions will result in 'Bringing the spirit if the game into disrepute'. Action should be taken immediately if the situation looks like escalating to violence, this unfortunately can happen.

ECCENTRICITIES

Fortunately most Umpires soon obtain a reputation for fairness which is as it should be and, indeed, some become known and loved for their eccentricities, these can endear them to players and spectators alike.

Many will recognize Umpire David Shepherd's familiar stance (hopping on one leg) when the score has reached 111, or 'Nelson' as it is known. This normally can signal for a wicket to fall to the superstitious.

Myself, I have fond memories of an old umpire of my acquaintance who regularly used to stand in the Wolverhampton area clubs matches. This old boy was well into his 70s when I was learning my craft over 25 years ago. He would be seen wearing the old style longer coat and sporting his old club cap. His coat would be held together with an ancient elastic 'Snake' belt and his lips were always firmly clamped around an equally ancient briar pipe. Being of advancing years he used to find it difficult at times to stand for a full match (up to 7 hours on your feet), so he affected to umpire while perched on a shooting stick. A great gentleman, a great umpire and a great character. God bless you old friend, wherever you are.

THE INTRODUCTION

Before the start of any match the Umpires and Scorers should introduce themselves to each other and if they are 'visiting' officials to the Captains of both teams playing.

THE CLAPPERS

When the Umpires are ready to take to the field (and they should be the first out on the field of play) they should ring the club bell, if one is available, to announce the early warning of commencement of play.

CHECKING THE PITCH

As the Umpires walk onto the field they should check that everything seems to be in place. It is the Umpires who place the bails on the stumps in readiness of the start of play.

THE COUNT

If you are umpiring make sure that you take a moment to look around you and count the players on the field. This may sound strange but I have encountered twelve men on the pitch not counting the Batsmen. It's always best to check.

DON'T FORGET THE SCORER

Before the Umpire at the Bowler's end calls out 'Play' to signal the start of the game, he should check to make sure that the Scorers are in place in the scoring box or wherever the designated scoring area is. I have known a match start with no one in place to score the runs! Unforgivable.

Also, the Umpire at the Bowler's end should signal to the Scorers and wait for them to acknowledge his signal that they are ready to commence.

After all this, with both Umpires in place, one at Bowler's end and one at square leg, the Bowler's end umpire can call out 'Play'. The game's afoot.

So, just to recap:

- Maintain dignity.

- Meet with your brother Umpire and Scorers before the match starts.

- Meet with both Captains.

- Check if there are any special arrangements to be taken into consideration.

- Check the condition of the pitch, particularly in bad weather.

- Make sure the wickets are in place.

- Place the bails on the wickets.

- Count the number of players on the field.

- Make sure your brother Umpire is in position.

- Check that the Scorers are ready.

Chapter 3
Signalling

The way an Umpire communicates to the Scorers and, indeed, to others watching the game is by the specially formulated signals. Use them! They were designed for this purpose. Signal clearly and always wait for the Scorers to acknowledge your signal. It can be so easy to signal and return to the game but the Scorers may not have seen your communication. Disaster!

Always remember that your signals convey information. A flourish when signalling a '4' for instance is quite acceptable but bear in mind that each signal has a purpose within it. Also, never use 'home grown' signals that only you know and never ever, no matter how badly provoked include hand gestures of the 'single finger' variety or worse. Many Scorers are ladies after all.

The signals that are used are simplicity itself. (You can check these signals on the chart shown).

BOUNDARY 4

If a ball is hit off a fair delivery by the Batsman and it travels unimpeded to the boundary line and either touches it or crosses it then the score shall be classed as '4'. The Umpire signals this by waving an arm across his body from left to right, his right arm is the most acceptable. At times this signal is the one that is customized by umpires with little flourishes. This is not a problem as long as the move is still recognizable as that prescribed by the laws of the game.

BOUNDARY 6

If the Batsman hits a ball off a fair delivery and it crosses the boundary line without touching the ground it is deemed to be a boundary '6'. The Umpire signals this by raising both arms in straight lines over his head.

BYE

When signalling a 'Bye', the Umpire should raise his right arm in a straight line to point skywards.

LEG BYE

This has caused me more amusement than any other signal used. If a 'Leg Bye' is signalled it should simply be a matter of the Umpire raising his right leg as if to climb an imaginary stair and then brush or tap his leg with his hand.

You would not believe the semi-balletic and even downright dangerous positions I have witnessed Umpires attain to signal this particular scoring phenomenon. Indeed, it has long been held by me that human beings are not built to obtain the configurations I have sometimes witnessed without permanent damage to themselves and uncontrollable hilarity in those observing.

WIDE

When the delivery is deemed by the Umpire to be 'Wide' he should stretch his arms out on each side of his body in a cruciform manoeuvre. It does help if the Umpire then calls out 'Wide Ball'; although this is not strictly in the laws it does assist the Scorer.

OUT

If the Umpire is asked 'How's that?' and he does believe that the Batsman is out, for one reason or another, he must signal the Batsman as being

Boundary 4

Boundary 6

Bye

Leg Bye

Wide

Out

Short run

Dead ball

No ball

Disregard
previous signal

'Out'. This is done by pointing in the direction of the Batsman in question somewhere in the region of the heavens above him, also saying clearly 'out' as to leave no doubt. If he finds the Batsman 'Not Out' he declares such.

Do not be tempted. Like an old colleague of mine who would not only signal in the prescribed manner but would, after a brief pause, make his finger point towards the clubhouse, adding insult to injury for the departing Batsman, amusing but hardly professional.

SHORT RUN

You should bend your arm upwards to touch your nearest shoulder repeatedly with the fingertips.

DEAD BALL

On certain occasions a ball will be deemed 'Dead'. To signal this the Umpire will place his hands crossed in front of himself and proceed to cross and uncross them, think dancing the Charleston and you will get the idea.

NO BALL

If a delivery is seen to be unfair for some reason the Umpire must raise his right arm at right angles to his body. This must be accompanied by the call of 'No Ball'. This signals to the Scorers and spectators that the delivery was seen as inadmissable.

DISREGARD PREVIOUS SIGNAL

This particular signal is not used much these days but it is perfectly legal and of great use to anyone engaged in the art of scoring. The style is simplicity itself.

Cross your chest with your arms as if adopting the pose of an Egyptian mummy. Then tap your shoulders with the hands of the opposing arms. Most efficacious, very stylish.

Please, if you are standing as an Umpire always make sure that the Scorer has seen your signal. Wait for the wave of recognition.

All of the reasons for these signals being given will be covered in the section dealing with the laws.

Let us now briefly revisit the matter of signals.

- Make your signals clear and precise.

- If a call is necessary make sure you call out in an audible manner.

- Make your signals in the direction of the Scorer's box.

- Wait for the Scorer's recognition.

THE
LAWS OF CRICKET

OFFICIAL

Marylebone Cricket Club

Chapter 4
Knowing the Laws

The laws of cricket are precise and in many cases complex. If you are not certain on a point ask, there is no dishonour in obtaining help, otherwise you run the risk of ruining the game with bad decisions.

Many cricket clubs provide training courses for umpires and scorers that run in the close season, attend them. They can only be beneficial to you, your club and therefore the game.

You will have noticed that I have used the term 'Laws', remember that cricket has laws other lesser games have rules.

The laws are in the custody of the MCC and can only be changed by expressed permission and much negotiation with this august body. The MCC, Marylebone Cricket Club, is the home of cricket and is sited at Lords Cricket Ground in London. Copies of the laws can be purchased from the shop there very reasonably and umpires and scorers would do well to obtain a copy. Where I have had to quote from the laws of the game the phrases are in quotation marks and clearly marked MCC at the end. I not only recognize the work done by the MCC in the world of cricket in general but I also freely recognize their ownership of the quotations I have used as belonging to the MCC.

Nobody can become an expert in the laws of cricket without training and dedication. The Association of Cricket Umpires and Scorers runs training courses which are designed for anyone who has an interest in pursuing this dedication.

An excellent book, considered by many to be the 'Bible' of the cricket game is 'Cricket Umpiring and Scoring' by Tom Smith. This is updated as the laws are redefined and is readily available in paperback. A must for any umpire and scorer.

Whereas the laws may be seen as complicated and obtuse to the uninitiated with study all can become clear. There are many laws that affect the game but here I will endeavour to provide those which I consider the most valuable for anyone who is either starting out or generally wishes to improve their knowledge of the game. For more detailed information please consider the publications I have just mentioned.

The laws even encompass:

- The Balls. (Please see the accompanying diagram).
- The circumference of the ball shall be no less than 22.4 cm, 8 $^{13}/_{16}$" circ.
- The ball shall be no more than 22.9 cm, 9" circ.
- The weight shall not be less than 155.9 g, 5 ½ oz.
- The weight shall not exceed 163 g, 5 ¾ oz.

There are interesting differences made for women's and junior cricket.

For women's cricket the weight shall not be less than 140 g, 4 $^{15}/_{16}$ oz.

- The weight shall not exceed 150 g, 5 $^{5}/_{16}$ oz.
- The size shall not be less than 8 ¼", 21 cm circ.
- The size shall not be more than 8 $^{7}/_{8}$", 22.5 cm circ.

For junior cricket the weight shall not be less than 133g, 4 $^{5}/_{16}$ oz.

- The weight shall not exceed 143 g, 5 $^{1}/_{16}$ oz.
- The size shall not be less than 8 $^{1}/_{16}$", 20.5 cm circ.
- The size shall not exceed 8 $^{11}/_{16}$", 22 cm circ.

All balls used during a match shall be approved by both Umpires and Captains.

LOST BALL

In the event of a ball becoming lost or unfit for play the Umpires shall allow a replacement ball that in their opinion is of a similar state of wear to the one lost. If a ball is to be replaced the Umpires shall inform the Batsmen.

NEW BALL

Subject to an agreement being made before the toss, either Captain may demand a new ball at the start of each innings. (Most leagues state this as part of their playing regulations).

Many times common sense prevails when it comes to replacement balls. We must remember that the average cricket ball is a very expensive item.

Although there are many styles available the laws still dictate the maximum sizes of:

- The Bat. (Please see the accompanying diagram).

- The width of an adult bat shall not be greater than 10.8 cm.

- The length of the bat shall not exceed 96.5 cm.

Many cricketers go to great lengths and have their bats made especially for them. It is of course perfectly acceptable to purchase one 'off the peg' at a sports shop. The weights vary considerably and many who play will choose either lighter or heavier models depending on their personal choice.

The famous Australian batsman Victor Trumper used a bat with an extra long handle and with a weight of 4 lbs, quite astonishing but in his hands lethal to England's bowlers.

My own bat is of a pattern used in the 1930s and weighs in at just under 2 lbs 10 ozs. God bless you 'Braddles' a super job. It is purely personal choice but the overall dimensions must comply with the laws.

When Umpires inspect the pitch and go out to look at the wicket they are also responsible for:

THE STUMPS AND BAILS

The laws state that the stumps or wickets shall be no more than 71.1 cm in length from the top when measured to the start of the tapered point which enters the ground.

The bails shall not be more than 11.1 cm in length.

The overall width of the assembled wicket (all three stumps and both bails in place) shall not exceed a width of 22.86 cm.

When we spoke earlier of the Umpire's equipment we mentioned using heavier bails in cases of high wind. Although the wood used is of heavier and denser material the overall dimensions still comply with the laws.

Law 3 clearly states that Umpires are to stand where they can best see any action that may require their adjudication.

This may seem clear but I would like to make a couple of points with regard to this.

There will be at any one time two Umpires on duty on the field of play.

The first will be called the 'Bowlers End' Umpire. He will stand behind the stumps from the end of the attacking Bowler. He may use his own personal judgement where he stands but it must not:

- Interfere with the Bowler's run-up and delivery.

- Impede the view of the Batsman on strike (getting ready to bat).

Stumps dimensions

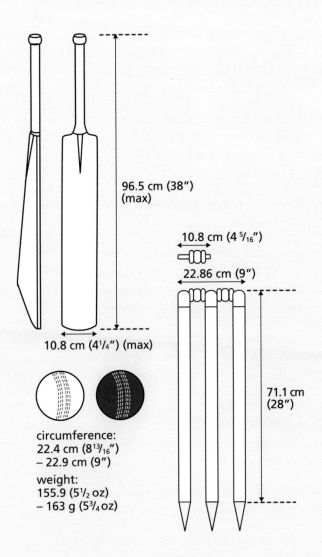

96.5 cm (38") (max)

10.8 cm (4 1/4") (max)

10.8 cm (4 5/16")

22.86 cm (9")

71.1 cm (28")

circumference:
22.4 cm (8 13/16")
– 22.9 cm (9")

weight:
155.9 (5 1/2 oz)
– 163 g (5 3/4 oz)

Normally this will be around four to six feet behind the stumps and level to the stumps. This will give him an unimpeded view of the Bowler's feet and of the areas of the wicket known as the 'popping' and 'return' creases.

The second of the officiating Umpires is called 'Square Leg' and he stands at the position on the field close by the square leg fieldsman. This normally means standing roughly the length of the pitch away from the Batsman on strike in line with the popping crease.

He should also have a clear view of the positioning of the Wicketkeeper. It may be required for him to give judgement from a keeper's appeal and this cannot be done if his view is not clear.

The square leg Umpire is sometimes called 'Strikers End' and this position is very often offered to young Umpires who are learning their craft.

Although the Umpires are normally needed to change positions alternately and at the end of each over, this is called by bowlers end when it is deemed that the over has been fairly completed. On some occasions when an Umpire is still inexperienced he will stay at square leg for the game and the more experienced will perform bowlers end throughout the match.

This is normally done due to the fact that in most matches the amount of appeals for decisions tends to be predominantly from the bowlers end. Thus allowing the 'rookie' to be inducted at a more gradual pace.

With this in mind I am brought back to my own period of training in the 1980s when at the first match I appeared in my white coat and I was offered and accepted square leg for the match. Indeed the bowlers end Umpire during this game was my old friend with the snake belt.

Imagine my surprise when as the match grew on virtually every appeal was for square leg Umpire; much to the amusement of my old friend.

At this match I was also taught a very sharp lesson in the matter of the Umpire not getting in the way of the ball. I firmly recall seeing the ball bowled and I certainly remember seeing it hit by the Batsman. However, imagine my chagrin when my next conscious thought is of lying on the ground, clutching my leg and being surrounded by my colleagues all of whom looked on with a mixture of concern and hilarity.

Always remember, get out of the way of the ball. They are hard and fast!

THE GAME'S AFOOT

After handing the match ball to the Bowler who will bowl first, the bowlers end Umpire can then assist in giving the Striker his guard. This is when the Striker (Batsman facing the bowler) will ask for help in positioning his bat in order to best protect his wicket. The Umpire will do this by gazing down the wicket as the Batsman places his bat on the ground to the position he has notified the Umpire of. This may be called by him as being 'One', 'Middle', 'Two', 'Leg', or any other configuration the Batsman desires. This is done because the Umpire has a clear and unobstructed view down the wicket to the Batsman. The Striker will then lightly mark the ground with his bat having been given the signal by the Umpire that his bat is in place.

The Bowler must give the Umpire information on the way he bowls, his style if you will. This may be 'Right arm over', 'Left arm round', or again any permutation he may devise. This detail is then given to the Striker by the Umpire.

Be warned however, any Bowler who does not give his action and bowls the first without doing so will be called 'No Ball' by the Umpire. This incurs a penalty to the bowling side, so all you young bowlers beware, you have duties too.

When the Umpire is satisfied that all is well with the world, or at least his little part of it, he then calls 'Play'; the game has now started.

OVER

Law 22. "The ball shall be bowled from each wicket alternately in overs of 6 or 8 balls according to the agreement before the match…

...When the agreed number of balls has been bowled and as the ball becomes dead the umpire shall call 'Over'. This signifies that the over is completed." MCC

Remember that a wide ball or a no ball will not be counted as part of that over but will be added as penalties to the score as will any runs scored off them.

When the Umpire has called 'Over', even if he has miscounted and has allowed only 5 balls, that over will stand as complete. The same applies if he allows 7 balls, once 'Over' is called the next commences from the facing wicket and the next Bowler comes on to ball.

A Bowler may bowl as many overs as he or she is capable of, at the discretion of the Captain. With junior cricket it is different and bowlers are limited as to the amount they may bowl but local youth leagues will furnish you with the information regarding this.

When the Bowler is delivering his balls the Batsman at his end of the wicket will stand to one side so as not to impede the Bowler's run up.

SCORING RUNS

For those of you who are not aware what a 'Run' is and here I must allow that some of you dear readers are perusing this as an introduction to the game, a run is counted when the Batsmen have run down the length of the pitch and made safe their ground after a ball has been bowled. You will be considered safe when your bat has crossed the line marked on the pitch in front of the wicket you have run towards.

BOUNDARIES

We have mentioned boundaries earlier, albeit briefly. A boundary is scored when the ball has been hit by a Batsman and it has travelled over the boundary marking the edge of the playing pitch.

If the ball runs along the ground and crosses the boundary it is called a '4' and it is scored accordingly. If the ball sails through the air and crosses the boundary without touching the ground first it is scored as '6' and again signalled accordingly. (See the Umpires signals for these).

Needless to say there are many permutations of these but as I mentioned earlier the Laws of Cricket will give you every possible angle on the rulings of these and other runs.

HATS OFF

A very interesting tangent on boundaries is the ruling regarding the Wicket Keeper's helmet. These days many keepers choose to wear a protective helmet while behind the stumps for their own safety, in some cases very wisely as there are some fine fast bowlers at club level.

During the game the keeper may feel the need to discard the helmet and when he takes it off it is customary for him to place it on the ground at some distance behind him. Now for a note of caution, if the ball is played by the Batsman and it travels down the pitch and should hit the helmet '5' runs are scored and the Umpire must signal this to the Scorers accordingly. Just holding up your hand with 5 fingers splayed is normally sufficient.

So keepers beware, wear your helmet but take it off and place it carefully.

DEAD BALL

This is a phenomena that many cricketers find confusing. I will first quote from the laws and then try and explain.

Law 23. "The ball becomes dead when:

- It is finally settled in the hands of the Wicket Keeper or Bowler.

- It reaches or pitches over the boundary.

- A Batsman is out.

- Whether played or not it lodges in the clothing of a player or Umpire.

- The Umpire calls over "Over" or "Time".

- Either Umpire can call "Dead Ball" when he intervenes in a case of unfair play.

- A serious injury occurs on the pitch to a player or Umpire.

- If the Striker is not ready when the ball is being delivered and makes no stroke to play it.

- Either or both of the bails fall from the wicket before the ball is bowled.

- The Striker leaves his ground for consultation.

The ball ceases to be dead when:

- The Bowler starts his run up or bowling action." MCC

This law always needs careful reading from the book of the laws. It is not particularly easy to determine unless you actually witness the events and many new umpires may sometimes and unwittingly fall into error on this point.

Always remember that if you think an action has occurred and reached its conclusion then the ball is probably dead.

Has a Batsmen been bowled or run out or been deemed out in some other way? Then the ball is dead until play resumes with a new Batsman.

Has the ball gone for a 4 or a 6? Then the ball is dead until the next ball is bowled.

Has the Wicketkeeper gathered the ball into his gloves after a delivery? Then the ball is dead.

Has the Bowler dropped the ball before bowling it? Then the ball is dead.

Have the bails been blown off or fallen off the stumps prior to a ball being bowled? Then the ball is dead.

But be warned. If the Bowler has started his run up and the non striking Batsman has started to back up his friend on strike and has left his safe ground the ball is not dead. Most certainly not and he can be run out by the Bowler with ball in his hand. Take care that in your enthusiasm this does not happen to you.

NO BALL

I have always looked on this as the cricket world's equivalent of the 'off side rule'. Many times I have heard the Umpire call 'No Ball', only to be replied to with a ubiquitous 'Ee woz neva'. I really must try and find out what that means one day!

Actually, like all things that are explained, the No Ball ruling is not complicated at all as long as you follow the guidelines.

Law 24. The method of delivery. Remember, we covered this one. The Umpire will indicate to the Striker whether the Bowler intends to bowl round or over the wicket, right- or left-handed and at one time whether he would bowl overarm or underarm (that's no longer the case, overarm is now the only official delivery).

The arm. The delivery will only be fair if the ball is bowled and not thrown. This means that the bowling arm must not be seen to be straightening out partially or fully prior to the time the ball leaves the hand.

The feet. This is down to the bowlers end Umpire. If the Bowler's back foot has not landed within and is not touching the return crease or its forward extension or some part of the front whether grounded or raised was behind the popping crease, he will call 'No Ball'. (Don't worry, look at the diagrams, then you can see it all at a glance.)

No ball

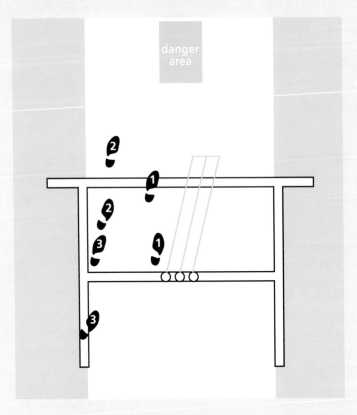

Position 1 is a fair delivery.

Position 2 is a no ball because no part of the front foot is behind the popping crease.

Position 3 is a no ball because the rear foot is touching the return crease.

The Wicketkeeper. Here is a chap who can incur a no ball as well. If the Keeper is standing up to the wicket to receive the ball being bowled, in other words if he is right behind the Batsman being bowled to, the Keeper must be aware that in his enthusiasm his hands do not encroach on the top of the bails to give him an unfair advantage of taking the wicket if he is attempting to dismiss the Batsman. On this occasion it is square leg Umpire who will call 'No Ball'.

Whether you are a player or an Umpire always remember that every time a no ball is called it is automatically 1 penalty 'run' and if the Batsmen decide to try and make runs on it they can do so but they are putting their wicket at risk. You can still be run out from a no ball, in fact there are a number of ways to be out from a no ball but again I will tell you to study further with your book of the laws.

If the Batsman hits the ball of a no ball and then makes runs from it, he will be granted the runs he has scored but not the penalty run for the no ball. Although it is scored it is shown as an extra but more of that in the scoring section.

If the Batsmen run off the no ball but the ball has not been hit then the score is still 1 penalty run and whatever they have accumulated in their running except that the batsmen will not get the runs accredited to them, they go down as 'Byes' and are signalled as such.

The Umpire must also remember that a no ball does not count as one of the six balls in an over, it counts as an extra ball and therefore one more ball must be bowled to make up for it. This can actually have disastrous effects; I recall one match which had no less than 7 no balls in the first over, this meant that 13 balls were bowled in that over alone, if my memory serves me I believe that the poor Bowler had 25 scored off him in that over (including the extras), something I know he would rather forget.

WIDE BALL

Law 25. Let's look at the wide ball now. This can be quite spectacular and always causes groans of agony from both the Bowler and the Wicket Keeper.

Here is how to judge a wide:

"If the bowler bowls the ball so high over or so wide of the wicket that the batsman can not reach it whilst in his normal guard position, the umpire will call it as wide." MCC

Again, there will be a run awarded as a penalty for this and again if the Batsmen decide to run for further runs they will all be counted but the Batsmen will not get the benefit on their personal scores. After all, they have hit nothing, why should they?

Once again, Batsmen remember if you put your wicket at risk while trying for runs off a wide ball you can still be out. Be warned.

BYE

Now here is a useful little extra, the 'Bye'. Please bear in mind that if 2 are scored it does not become a bye-bye!

Law 26. "If the ball, not being called either wide or no ball, passes the Striker without touching his bat or person and any runs are obtained from this the Umpire will signal all runs from this as 'Byes'. The batting side get the benefit but not the individual batsmen." MCC

I recall many, many years ago when in my enthusiasm for the game I attended one complete season scoring for a club in the Midlands and for the whole season I gave each batsman the byes he had scored throughout the whole year. The averages were superb, the figures looked stupendous, my name, however, was mud!

The 'Leg Bye' is similar. Again if the ball is not called wide or no ball and is unintentionally deflected off the Batsman's clothing or equipment, except the hand holding the bat, any runs scored off that are called as leg byes. Once again, the team gets the runs, not the individual.

These are the scourge of the Wicket Keeper as he will valiantly try to prevent any runs being scored off them and the Bowler will always be in a state of remorse for making the Keepers job even more difficult.

APPEALING OR APPALLING?

An Umpire must not give any judgement unless he is asked. This is called answering an appeal. You will normally hear the cry of 'How's that?' frequently heard as 'Owzatt' or 'Owizee'. The Umpire can then give his assessment.

Remember you can only give a Batsman out if you are asked and if there is any doubt, any doubt at all in your mind as to whether or not the Batsman is indeed out you must find for the Batsman, he must be deemed by you as 'Not Out'.

Bear in mind that if you are standing as an Umpire and there is a point you are not certain of, or your view has for some reason been obstructed, you may and indeed must consult with your brother Umpire. There is no shame in this. Remember, when in doubt shout!

WHAT ABOUT A WICKET BEING DOWN?

Law 28. "A wicket is considered down if the bails are removed in some way from the standing stumps." MCC

This can happen in any number of ways, sometimes with spectacular results. Even if one bail is knocked or dislodged off the stumps it is sufficient to deem that wicket as down.

If the ball is bowled fairly and knocks off the bail or bails, then of course the Batsman is out bowled. If the Batsman should by accident and while taking his stroke knock off the bails then again he is out. This used to be called 'Played On' but now it is deemed bowled. If the Wicket Keeper knocks off the bails while the Batsman is out of his ground then he has been 'Stumped', this is the great achievement of any Keeper and one of which they are all rightly proud.

At times the bails are dislodged literally by accident, the wicket is considered broken and the game can not continue until the bails are safely back in place. The Umpire at square leg normally does this and so the game can continue.

TIMED OUT

This is a rare occurrence but one that does happen sometimes. In local club cricket it is only enforced by those who are sticklers for the laws, but they are quite correct in doing so as it is after all a law of the game.

Law 31. "An incoming Batsman shall be timed out if he or she 'wilfully' takes more than two minutes to come in to bat. The two minutes is timed from the moment the wicket falls until the new Batsman steps onto the field of play." MCC

The emphasis here is on the word 'wilfully' and it is the Umpire's duty to oversee this. Once again, however, an appeal must be made for this to be judged and the Umpire must then judge according to his reading of the situation.

WHAT IF SOMEONE IS CAUGHT?

This is a very common form of dismissal and it means that the Batsman who is on strike has hit the ball with his bat or if it touches the wrist, hand or glove holding the bat and that the ball is then subsequently caught by a fieldsman before it touches the ground.

2000 wickets (or more) in a career

	Name	Career	Wickets	Runs
1.	W Rhodes	1898-1930	4187	69993
2.	A P Freeman	1914-36	3776	69577
3.	C W L Parker	1903-35	3278	63817
4.	J T Hearne	1888-1923	3061	54352
5.	T W J Goddard	1922-52	2979	59116
6.	W G Grace	1865-1908	2876	51545
7.	A S Kennedy	1907-36	2874	61034
8.	D Shackleton	1948-69	2857	53303
9.	G A R Lock	1946-71	2844	54709
10.	F J Titmus	1949-82	2830	63313

The fielder catching the ball must be within the boundary area though. If he catches the ball and is over the boundary then that boundary has been scored by the Batsman.

Always remember though that if the ball touches the ground then that is not a catch, the Batsman is not out.

CAUGHT BEHIND

This happens when a Batsman plays his shot and then the ball is caught, again without touching the ground, behind him, normally by the Keeper. You can also be caught by Slips and Gully. There you are, you always thought slips were an article of lingerie and gullies collected rainwater didn't you?

A variation on this is fabulous 'Stumping', so beloved of the Wicketkeeper. This occurs when the Striker has left his ground and is playing a shot but the ball has come into the Keeper's gloves. If the Keeper is quick enough he can then knock off the bails with the hands holding the ball and if the Batsman is out of his ground then he is out stumped.

This takes razor sharp reflexes on the part of the Keeper and is the pinnacle of his game. If you are umpiring however you must keep your eyes peeled for this one. If the Batsman is even on the line of his crease then he is out. The line marks the Keeper's victory. The Batsman must be inside it, on it is not good enough. Also, just check, did the hand that took off the bails hold the ball? They must be removed by the gloved hands holding the ball, nothing else will do.

LEG BEFORE WICKET

Now here is a beauty. Every Umpire must pay particular attention to this. This occurs when a ball is bowled and travels down the pitch towards the Batsman and strikes the Batsman's person. The official explanation is as follows:

Law 36. "The Striker shall be out LBW if he first intercepts with any part of his person, dress or equipment a fair ball which would have hit the wicket

Leg before wicket

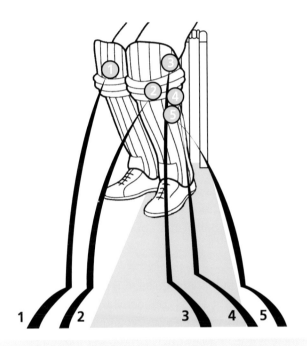

1 Not out. The ball has struck the pad well outside the line of the stumps (and the batsman offered a shot).

2 Probably not. The umpire may rule not out if he thinks the ball was turning sharply enough to miss the stumps.

3 Possibly not. The umpire may rule not out if he thinks the ball was rising sharply enough to clear the stumps.

4 Out. The ball pitched in line with the stumps and would have gone on to hit them.

5 Not out. The ball pitched outside leg-stump.

and which has not previously touched his bat or a hand holding the bat provided that:

The ball pitched in a straight line between wicket and wicket or on the off side of the striker's wicket or was intercepted full pitch. Or the point of impact is in a straight line between wicket and wicket, even if above the level of the bails." MCC

The Striker will also be out LBW even if the ball is intercepted outside the line of the off stump if, in the opinion of the Umpire, he has made no attempt to play the shot but has intercepted the ball with some part of his person and if the other circumstances stated earlier apply.

Now my friends, it's not as bad as it sounds. Just study the diagram and all will be clear. If you are umpiring you would be astonished at how many Batsmen will argue the toss over this one. Always remember, stand your ground, stand by your decision but above all, if again there is any doubt at all in your mind then the Batsman is not out.

RUN OUT

As I mentioned earlier in this little guide, it is only possible for me to give you the bare outline of the laws I consider you should master to understand the game better, whether you be a young umpire in training or just a keen spectator. There is one more I would like to cover though before I finish the section on umpiring.

Law 38. This law deals with the run out. The laws state that "Either Batsman shall be run out if in running or at any time while the ball is in play he is out of his ground and his wicket is put down by the opposite side. If however a Batsman makes good his ground then he shall be not out." MCC

If the Batsmen have crossed in running he who runs for the wicket which is put down shall be run out. If they have not crossed he who has left the wicket that is put down shall be run out. If the Batsmen have run one run successfully and are returning for a second and then a wicket is put down, only the first completed run is to be scored. The attempted run in which the run out occurred shall not be counted.

Actually, it's rather simple. Nothing to give you sleepless night there. If you are umpiring and this happens, try to be in a position to see the line of the crease, no not try you must see the line of the wicket to give a judgement. Keep your eyes peeled, if the Batsman's bat makes his ground he is not out. Watch out for the toe of his bat, even if it is on the line marking his ground he is not safe, he must be inside.

NEW LAWS FOR OLD

Always keep an eye on the updating of laws. This happens frequently and you should check before the start of the season to ascertain if any laws have come into being that may affect the game at your level.

BRIGHT EYES

A new law has been passed that will affect all umpires. When it comes to the question of 'Bad Light' it will now not be the case of the umpire offering the choice of batting on to the batsmen at the crease. From the start of the 2011 season the umpires will make the decision and the teams must comply. Oh my, I can hear the tacticians bewailing now.

HEADS?

The toss has also been affected. Now it is necessary for at least one umpire to be present at the toss. The winning captain (of the toss) must then inform his counterpart of his decision to either bat or field immediately. Previously it has been acceptable for the winning captain to be able to wait for up to ten minutes before doing this.

DIGGING FOR VICTORY

We have all seen them. The batsmen who not only mark their crease but who appear to be preparing a celery trench! All this will now change. The umpire is now empowered to give just one warning to the offender before any penalty runs are awarded.

HOME DELIVERY SERVICE

Bowlers beware. If bowling and your front foot has crossed the imaginary line between the middle stumps the umpire will call! For example, you may have declared that you are bowling over the wicket but this action will effectively mean you have bowled round the wicket. No balls abound!

WASTE NOT WANT NOT

If you are used to bowling the ball into the ground to a team mate you are in peril. You will now be called for either damaging the ball or time wasting.

PRACTICE MAKES PERFECT

But not during a match! You will no longer be able to practise with either a coach or twelfth man outside the boundary during the game. This will now be seen as an opportunity to practise that is not available to the batsmen in the middle.

BEWARE SHRAPNEL

Law 28.1 has been amended to cope with an unusual but possible action. If the batsman is making a stroke and his bat breaks during the making of this shot, he will be deemed out if any part of his broken bat hits the stumps.

GROUNDED

Law 29.1 has also been amended. This will protect a batsman who is within his ground but whose feet or bat are in the air at the moment his bails are removed. He will now be deemed 'In'.

Well dear reader, that is as far as I will go on the subject of umpiring. There is much more that can be written on this and indeed has been. I hope in the space allotted to me I have perhaps cleared up some of your questions on the laws that I have been able to cover. As I mentioned earlier, for more detailed information on this matter obtain 'Cricket Umpiring and Scoring' by Tom Smith. It is worth its weight in gold to the aspiring Umpire or Scorer.

So, just to recap this section:

- Stand in a position where you have a good view but do not obstruct the field of play or the Bowler.

- You must remain focused at all times, a moment's lapse can cost a wicket.

- Answer appeals fairly and firmly.

- Do not be afraid to consult with your brother Umpire.

- Make sure your signals are seen and recognized by the Scorers.

- If you have any doubt about an appeal find in the favour of the Batsman.

- Keep your eyes peeled for any law infringements.

- In short be a super-human demigod. That's all there is to it.

" That was a tremendous six. The ball was still in the air as it went over the boundary. "

Fred Trueman

Part Four
Scoring

Chapter 1
Basic Requirements

Whether you are a willing recruit to the noble art of scoring or even if you are one of the 'press-ganged' masses that are called upon to perform this task you have certain duties to perform, perform them to the best of your ability.

Be vigilant, precise, clear and keep an eye on the Umpire at all times. These super human feats can form the balance between a well kept book and potential disaster when deciding on scores in a close run game when even 1 run can decide success or failure for a team.

You do not need to have an aptitude for mathematics, in fact I would class myself as being most 'unmaths-like' in temperament. All you need to do is try to stay calm and record things as they happen in the manner prescribed.

It has been said that all a Scorer has to do is to score the runs as they occur and to acknowledge the Umpire's signals. All? Good grief, if it were only that simple.

Yes, the scoring and recording of the runs and falls of wicket is of paramount importance, but if you want to do more, to become a really proficient Scorer, then there is far more you can do.

As with umpiring you should at least be interested in the duty you have undertaken. Even if you are a player who has been seconded to keep the book whilst waiting to go in to bat, or if you are a Batsman who is out and is keeping the book to avoid boredom, at least try to do it with interest and enthusiasm.

In other words, be the best you can be. Do your best for the boys, or girls, keep the book well.

Something to keep in mind is that a Scorer can be anyone. Young or old, male or female. Just as long as they love the game.

Scoring is also a very good way to introduce youngsters to the game as well as giving a superb pastime for those who have retired from active cricket and who do not wish to Umpire or are unable to stand due to inability.

THE SCORER'S EQUIPMENT

PENCILS

If you are a beginner at scoring use a pencil. Remember ink is permanent, pencil is easily erased. Even if you are experienced in the calling always have sharpened pencils with you, it's always possible to have an off day and then the graphite is your friend.

Even for the most experienced of Scorers mistakes can happen. If you are using pen then always carry the ubiquitous 'Tipp-ex'. Not only does it eradicate mistakes but, if sniffed it makes a slow afternoon pass reasonably painlessly!

On the subject of pencils, choose carefully, may I suggest the type classed as HB for those of you not yet experienced. The lead is softer and will leave a good mark on the paper.

You may after a while like to use a harder lead, this is fine but be warned, do not use a lead so hard as to make it difficult to read once used.

A good pencil sharpener is of great importance and should be chosen with care. I would suggest that you purchase the sort that are encased in a type of canister, these keep the pencil shavings from falling all over your clothing or the floor of the score box.

A rubber too is indispensable. You should always use one that is of a softer quality. The hard types, such as those that can erase ink can actually tear the paper of the page you are scoring on, or, at the very least, rub the page into a type of pilling such as one experiences on poor knitwear.

THE MOVING FINGER WRIT

After a time and if you feel confident enough, then by all means use pens. Always remember that with a pen once you have written the number or word needed, it is there for eternity (failing the use of Tipp-ex).

THE DREADED BALLPOINT

As to the type of pens you should use. This has to be done very carefully. One thing I would suggest is that you never, ever, use the type commonly called 'Ballpoint'. Whereas the pen may feel comfortable and this is always something you should keep in mind, the problem comes with the type of ink used in these particular pens.

ACID REIGN?

All ballpoint pens use an ink that is not of the type that can be described as 'archive sound'. Allow me to explain. The ink has within it an acid and fixative that allows the solid ink to flow and adhere to the paper. Unfortunately this acid fixative will, in time, eat through the paper. I do not mean that you will one day pick up your book and find it harassed and subdued with denture marks. What you will find is that, after a few years, the ink will be seen through the pages and throughout the book. You will be looking at one page and the previous and subsequent will be visible through them.

THE POSTERITY QUESTION

This may not seem like such a big deal, but when you remember that the score book is the permanent record of the club for all ages does it not make sense for you to take the care to ensure that it is still visible to future generations?

This being said ballpoints are very useful for cleaning out the ears of errant poodles!

FABULOUS FIBRE

I have found the best type of pen to use are those of the fine fibre tip variety. Possibly the very best are those produced by Staedtler and Pilot, although the latter are of French manufacture and some might argue that using a French product on an English cricket score book is heresy. Grit your teeth dear Scorer and remember Agincourt!

Obviously if you are going to use pens you must also look at the size of the point of the pen you are going to be scoring with. Over the years I have used many types and have found that two types of pen are best employed together when scoring in a book to best advantage.

CHOOSE CAREFULLY

First I always like to choose a slightly broader pen filling in the match details, such as club names, Batsmen's and Bowlers' names and details etc. For the actual scoring process I have found that a point size of '01' is the most effective.

NEITHER A BORROWER

Be warned, you will be asked by Captains and the like, particularly if they are filling out a batting order list, to lend them a pen. For heaven's sake, make sure you carry an ordinary pen with you for these occasions. Lending someone a fine point pen used for scoring can only end in tears. Many of mine came back with the tips all bent out of shape and impossible for their designed use.

PAPER CHOICES

Something to keep in mind when choosing pens is the type of book you are to use. In fact I would advise any Scorer to be present at the choosing of the book. These days, many are made from recycled paper. I applaud this but sometimes it can have an adverse effect on the scoring of a game.

The paper when reconstituted can become over absorbent. This results in the paper soaking up too much ink at any one time with the result that the numbers or letters written down tend to 'spider' across the page. This is dreadful, and should be avoided at all costs.

CHOOSING YOUR BOOK

I suggest that when you buy a score book you use the same type that has previously been acceptable for the club you score for. It is even a thought to take an old score book with you when buying pens, in this way you can try out new pens on the back of your old book to make sure that the ink and paper are compatible.

If you are in any doubt as to the proper type of paper in the books you are looking at follow the simple rule that if the pages are very matt or 'hairy', you know what I mean, then the ink might spider. If the pages are smoother or with a slight eggshell finish you are in with a better chance.

Obviously, the better the paper, the better the finish.

A MATTER OF TASTE. THE COLOURS QUESTION

There are many Scorers of my acquaintance who score 'in colours', this can look superb. In fact when you view a book that has been kept in this manner the effect is stunning and will always draw comments of compliment from those viewing it.

Now whereas this is very good to see, you must make sure that all the pens are from the same manufacturer. The inks must be comparable for quality and you must also have enough of a selection to cover any eventuality that may occur. This can mean 12 pens of varying shades in a similar ink quality and point size. Get this wrong and the effect is lost.

I recall one scoring colleague of mine who turned up at my club to score with me, not in the biblical sense you understand, and he proceeded to produce a box of every type of colour pen you can think of. Scheherazade's wardrobe never looked so fabulous. He duly marked all the Bowlers' names down in a different colour, but as the game progressed he proceeded to fill in their bowling analysis in black ink. The whole point of using colour is that you can trace the Bowler's progression through the match by following his colour. Imagine my shock, imagine my bemusement, imagine my hilarity.

CORRECTION FLUID. NOT TO BE SNIFFED AT!

As I mentioned earlier, using ink will by means of necessity mean that one day you will have to correct an error. Correction fluid I love you! Tipp-ex is the most common but there are numerous variances out there.

It is possible to obtain correction pens, I have had problems with these, the tips seem to clog easily and the fluid is unreliable. Correction tape is actually rather good. It is applied by a sort of mini sellotape dispenser and very neat it is as well, perfectly suitable for correcting larger areas such as names, etc but for detail I still maintain that the liquid is best.

CHECK THE SURFACE

Whereas the liquid correction is first rate, you might want to invest in a bottle of thinner to accompany it. The fluid can thicken and dry up in time. Thinner allows it to be kept longer. Again, before you settle on a brand of correction try out the various options.

Some will only accept ballpoint after application. Others take longer to dry. And, of course, some don't smell as good as others.

One word of warning though, no matter how dire the game gets never drink the thinners, not a good idea even with tonic!

Also take care in very hot weather. Admittedly the occasion is rare in England but I recall being in a score-box during a particularly hot day and the temperature in the box rose to 33 celsius. Imagine my horror when my bottle of fluid actually exploded quite spectacularly halfway through the first innings and covered the book, the table, me and most of my colleague with its rapidly stiffening contents. Keep it wrapped in a little plastic cash bag. Much safer.

KEEP IT CLEAR

We have spoken of using colours for scoring. I love to see it done properly but myself I tend to use plain black for details with red for special information. In fact most county Scorers only use black. I rather like the contrast of red and black, it's very pleasing to the eye and makes the specialist detail stand out, at least in my view.

For the areas of the book that need written words I use the slightly broader points. Black for club details, blue for Batsmen's and Bowlers' names, etc and red for the methods of dismissal (How Out). For the rest it's down to my beloved 01 points.

YOUR BOX

Alright, we have all heard of the cricket box, or 'Sport Support' as I believe it is now called. Actually at one of my old clubs we had a pre-war wicket keepers abdominal protector. This thing was vast with large straps and a monstrous panelled front. It was known fondly as 'Darth Vader'. It certainly would not be out of place in the male equivalent of an Anne Summers catalogue (or so I'm told)!

KEEPING SPARES

Anyway, back to the scorer's box and here I don't mean the one you sit in but the one you carry your pens and pencils in. I know it sounds strange, any old bag will do won't it? No it won't! If you're going to do the job properly then get the right kit. I always carry two. One is a super old wooden pencil case with a sliding top and I use it for my pens, the second is a tin for spare pens and pencils. Always carry spares, you never know when an accident will happen. Plus, it's worth keeping in mind that a visiting Scorer could have had an accident and lost or damaged their own pens, then you are on hand to help. That's what it's all about. You are a Scorer, another Scorer is by definition your colleague and associate and, believe me, as the seasons progress your friend. Over the years I have made many friends with whom I am still in touch, after all you sit next to each other for about 7 hours at a time, you'd better be friends and quickly!

THE RIGHT BAG

It can also be very useful to purchase some type of bag to keep your scoring kit in. Personally I favour a 'bowling' bag, you know, the sort they keep bowls in! It provides room for all my pens and pencils as well as the other items I carry.

In fact let's talk about things to carry with you.

Apart from my two pen/pencil boxes and my small bag for my correction fluid I also find it very useful to carry the following:

- Spare bails (just in case).

- Spare ball (ditto).

- Beer towels (2 is enough).

- Spare boot studs (players can lose them easily).

- Boot stud spanner.

- White boot laces.

- Abdominal protector (you never know)!

- A copy of the MCC Laws.

- A spare scoring book with detachable pages.

- A travel alarm clock.

- A pair of binoculars (a monocular is just as good).

- My cricket sweater (club colours of course).

- A calculator (sometimes our brain can seize up).

- Sunglasses (live in hope of getting some sun).

The boys at my club call it the 'Doctor's bag'. I always like to be ready for any eventuality.

KEEPING THE LAWS

The copy of the laws is always of use in case there is a dispute and the Umpire has forgotten his. Spare bails for the same reason. The spare book is in case the team you are playing forget theirs, believe me this happens with astonishing regularity.

WHY CARRY SO MUCH?

Your pencil case should also contain spares for the same reason. The travel alarm is always good to have on the table in front of you, set to the agreed time of course. Always carry your sweater, it can get extremely cold at games at the start and the end of the season. In fact, while we are at it, bung in a hip flask! Now you are sure to make friends.

This might all sound excessive but believe me there will be times when people are running around like the proverbial headless chickens looking for items that have been lost or forgotten. Step in to the breach, you are the Scorer!

Congratulations, you are all set. Now let us look at the methods of scoring and the books available.

Chapter 2
Methods of Scoring

There are many types of scoring styles open to the aficionado. These can vary from the simplest of books in which the most basic information is stored to the extremely detailed in which every ball of the game can be timed and noted. Choose the right one for you and make sure you are comfortable with it. Why not go with your club captain when he or she goes buying equipment. See the choices available and make your decision.

SEE WHAT'S AVAILABLE

Most of the books that are available are very self-explanatory and require little study before use. In this section of the book you will find I have used two quite simple layouts that are perfect for anyone starting scoring and even efficacious for the more experienced Scorer.

The book may be simple and I suggest your first one should be, but the information you can show in the book is endless. You do not need a large 'all singing, all dancing' version to do a good job.

WHICH STYLE OF BOOK TO CHOOSE

There are two basic forms of scoring, the most popular 'Box' scoring and then you have the 'Linear' method. I always use the box system; I am comfortable with it and frankly after all these years I still find the linear method confusing. Most county Scorers still use the box method and it serves the purpose very well. Maybe I'm just getting old and resistant to change. Getting old? I hear you exclaim in horror, ah dear reader the eyes are sharp, the fingers nimble but new tricks do not come easily.

THE COMPUTER AGE

In some clubs they have even adopted the very highest levels of the computer age into their scoring. All very well and good but it takes away the art of scoring I feel. The information is very correct, if it is put in correctly but it lacks the flourish of the human hand and pen. But that is only my opinion and I still embrace my computerized colleagues as friends and merely contain myself to a soft chuckle as their batteries run out half way through the second innings.

So, you have your new score book in front of you and your pencils or pens are neatly arranged for use. Let's start scoring.

YOUR STYLE OF SCORING

Every type of scoring technique I mention you will be able to check in the illustrations you will find in this text.

You may wish to start simply by showing the runs scored by each Batsman and then recording the same in the Bowlers area on the page. This along with the running total and fall of wicket information is quite adequate. You can always expand later into other avenues of providing details.

Let me explain what I mean.

FILLING IN THE DETAILS

You have filled in the names of both clubs at the top of your scoring page. You have asked who has won the toss and who will be batting first. You have introduced yourself to the Umpires and you have asked the Captain of the batting side for a batting order (the list of batsmen as they are to go to the wicket). Here is the first possible pitfall. If you are using pencil fair enough but if you are using pen beware, the Captains are notorious for changing the batting order leaving you with names filled out and a plethora of Tipp-ex to play with. I suggest that you only fill out the first four or five and then leave the rest until necessary.

THE SECOND SCORER

Also are you the only one scoring? This is not a good idea. There should always be two Scorers at any one time. If the team you are playing has not brought a Scorer then introduce yourself to the Captain and ask if you can have volunteers from his side to help keep their book. When they are in the field ask your team mates to assist you in similar fashion. If you do this, always ask the visiting Captain if he will accept your figures at the end of the day; this is covering yourself in case of a discrepancy with their book. Apart from that it gives you a professional look in the face of the visitors, always a good thing to inspire confidence.

THE PLAYERS DETAILS

You should now also have the names of the first two Bowlers and have been told which ends they will be bowling from, always good, you might not know them by sight. If for some reason you do not know a player's name and the person you have seconded to score with you does not, write down, in pencil only, a short description. 'Tall, fast, wearing long sleeved sweater' etc, you can then fill out the name at a later stage.

LET'S SCORE AN OVER

You will find a box on the Batsmen's analysis that says 'Time In and Time Out'. When the Umpire calls 'Play' fill out the time for the first two Batsmen. The Bowler will now start his run up and bowl the ball to Batsman number 1. It is a fair delivery, you were hoping for that!, and no run is taken, you just put a single dot in the Bowler's box, top left and corner. The ball is sent back to the Bowler who goes back to his marker and starts his run up again, he delivers the ball again fairly and this time the Striker hits it and starts to run. He reaches the other end of the wicket and Batsman number 2 is now facing. All you have to do, in this simplest form of scoring is to make sure that you put down a number 1 in the 1st Batsman's analysis and a number 1 in the Bowler's box. Each time a run is scored go over to the accumulative total, this is a large box containing numbers, normally 0-399 and it is normally found on the right of your page. Just tick off the amount of runs scored each time. This is there to show you the running total and helps keep the book in a state of self-checking.

YOU'RE HALFWAY THERE

The ball is returned to the Bowler and he commences his run up for his 3rd delivery. He bowls the ball to Batsman number 2 who is now Striker and he hits the ball and starts to run. Batsman 1 is also running and this time they complete two runs so that Batsman 2 is once again Striker. Place a number 2 against the Batsman and a 2 in the Bowler's box.

After the ball has been returned to the Bowler he commences his run up again. The ball travels down the wicket and the Batsman plays it down, he makes no playing stroke. Just put a single dot in the Bowlers box in the top right hand corner.

The Bowler bowls his 5th ball and the Striker (Batsman 2) hits it for a boundary. The ball goes past the fielders and reaches the boundary travelling on the ground and the Umpire signals a 4. Don't panic. Just wave back at the Umpire to let him know you've seen him and put a 4 in the Batsman's analysis and a 4 in the Bowler's box under the last dot.

Here comes the 6th ball. It travels to the Striker and he plays it down again. The Umpire calls 'Over' and you have just completed your first scoring over. Well done!

FINISHING THE OVER

You will see on your page, normally at the bottom or sometimes on the side a series of boxes that say Overs, Score, Wickets and sometimes Bowler as well. Just put in the score, which at this point is 7 and no wickets have fallen. The Bowler is number 1 and the first over is completed.

Don't forget to add up any runs in the over and write them down in the small section under the Bowler's box. As each over is completed you will add these together in an aggregate.

THE NEXT OVER

You are now ready for over number 2. This time a second Bowler comes on from the other end and facing him is Batsman number 1, if you remember they changed ends during the last over. Just watch and proceed as you have in the previous over. Nothing can go wrong, I have faith in you.

NOTING THE BOUNDARIES

Let us assume that a miracle happens and the innings continues with no fall of wicket and no extras. You've just got lucky! But what about those boundaries? Don't look at the ball. Watch the umpire. I have seen many scorers who have almost leant out of the score box trying to see what has happened to the ball, don't bother, the Umpire will tell you if it has gone for a 4 or 6. Keep your eye on him and just count the number of times the Batsmen run between the wickets in case no boundary occurs. Mark the runs in the book and all will be well.

Ok! You've come this far, let's look at extras and what to do if you get the signals I have described in the previous section from the Umpire.

THE EXTRAS

NO BALL

If the Batsman hits it and runs are scored off his shot you will allow him his runs and put 1 in the No Ball section of the Extras box. You will also draw a small circle, in it you will place the amount of runs the Batsman has run. This circle goes in the Batsman's analysis and in the Bowler's box as well. Don't forget, there will be an extra ball in the over for this.

If the Batsman does not hit the ball but runs anyway you will do the same except that in the circle you will put the same number of dots that the Batsmen have run. Again this goes in the Bowler's box and the Batsman's analysis. The Umpire will signal 'Byes' to you if this happens so that you will know the Batsman has not hit the ball.

THE WIDE BALL

This one is even easier. If the ball is Wide the Umpire will signal it to you and probably call as well. Just count the amount of times the Batsmen run, if they do, and this time you draw a small cross. You put a dot in each corner of the cross for any runs, if there are no runs then the cross is plain. Once again this goes against the Bowler and Batsman facing it. Don't forget to put the amount of runs, if any, in the Wides Box, if no runs are counted then just 1 goes in. Yet again one more ball will be allowed in the over to allow for the wide.

You see? Nothing to fret about at all.

BYES AND LEG BYES

The Umpire will signal as I mentioned earlier. You will only have to put a dot in the Bowler's box for either of these and put whatever is run off them in the box marked Bye or Leg Bye. Don't forget to place them on the accumulative score too.

ACKNOWLEDGE THE UMPIRE

I can't stress enough that while all this is going on you must answer the Umpire's signals. If you do not the result is a somewhat manic dance by a man in a white coat resembling the precursor to an attack by a Masai warrior. Be kind, don't wear him out!

MORE WORK?

Why not. We have come this far let us go even further in supplying information. Remember, this is not necessary but it gives you a sense of kudos and is also a boon to your club.

SCORING A CATCH

If the bowler has bowled the ball and it has been played by the Batsman it may be that he is 'Caught' by another player in the field. As well as following the standard procedure try this:

Around the dot for the ball played place a letter C denoting he has been caught. That dot should then become a W as his wicket has fallen. If any runs have been made before the catch has been taken then place the C around the number. Place the same in the Bowler's analysis.

TILLER GIRLS (A BEVY OF LEGS)

If the ball is bowled and as it hits the Striker's body an appeal for Leg Before Wicket is called then place a letter L around the ball in question by the Batsman's analysis and again for the Bowler. If the appeal is given then the dot again becomes a W signifying the fall.

TEFLON FINGERS

Ok, I know this is taking things a bit far but we have come a long way and I think you can do it!

If we now assume the ball has been bowled and that the Striker has hit it, what can we do if the then attendant attempt at a catch is dropped? Simple? We can place an inverted C underneath the dot to denote it, this can also be placed underneath any number that can result if runs are taken from the ball. The fielder will hate you, posterity will love you. Make your choice.

GET READY FOR TEA

At the end of an innings if no wickets have fallen you must still complete the page prior to you taking tea (actually I always do this quickly in pencil, especially if there is Chinese Battenburg cake on the table). Always be sure to mark the time the innings has finished, you remember it's in the section by the Bowlers' names you used at the start of the match.

BATTING ANALYSIS

To the right of the Batsmen's page you will find another series of boxes. These say 'How Out', 'Bowler' and 'Total'. In the first box write 'Not Out', if there is no fall of wicket they are both Not Out. Then in the box marked 'Total' you put the amount of runs each Batsman has scored against his name.

Sample score sheet

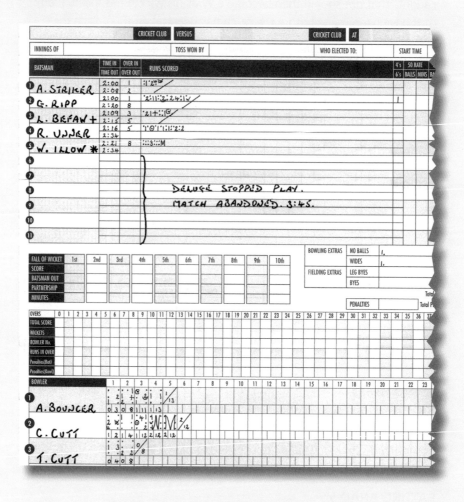

Wide = $+$ $\overset{\cdot}{+}$ $\overset{\cdot\cdot}{+}$ $\overset{\cdot\cdot}{\underset{\cdot}{+}}$ $\overset{\cdot\cdot}{\underset{\cdot\cdot}{+}}$ 1, 2, 3, 4 runs not hit

No ball = ◯ ① ② ③ ④ 1, 2, 3, 4 runs off bat

⊙ ⊙⊙ ⦂⦂ ⦂⦂ 1, 2, 3, 4 runs not hit

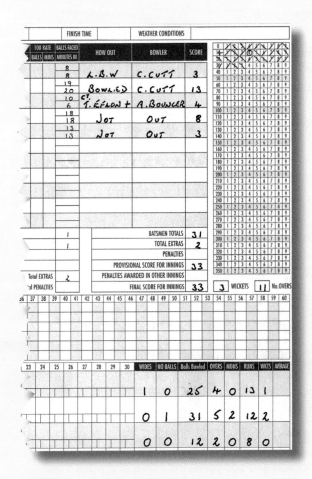

	FINISH TIME		WEATHER CONDITIONS		

100 RATE		BALLS FACED	HOW OUT	BOWLER	SCORE
BALLS	MINS	MINUTES IN			
		8 / 8	L.B.W	C. CUTT	3
		19 / 20	BOWLED	C. CUTT	13
		10 / 6	CT. T. EFLON †	A. BOUNCER	4
		18 / 18	NOT	OUT	8
		13 / 13	NOT	OUT	3

	BATSMEN TOTALS	31
	TOTAL EXTRAS	2
	PENALTIES	
	PROVISIONAL SCORE FOR INNINGS	33
	PENALTIES AWARDED IN OTHER INNINGS	
Total EXTRAS 2	FINAL SCORE FOR INNINGS	33

Total PENALTIES

3 WICKETS 11 No. OVERS

	WIDES	NO BALLS	Balls Bowled	OVERS	MDNS	RUNS	WKTS	AVERAGE
	1	0	25	4	0	13	1	
	0	1	31	5	2	12	2	
	0	0	12	2	0	8	0	

Wicket = **W** Ⓦ ─┼ᵂ   wicket, off no-ball, off wide

Bye = ◇1 ◇2 ◇3 ◇4   1, 2, 3, 4 runs

Leg Bye = ☐1 ☐2 ☐3 ☐4   1, 2, 3, 4 runs

BOWLERS' ANALYSIS

At the bottom of the page and to the right of the Bowler's section, you will see boxes marked 'Overs', 'MDNS', 'Runs', 'WKTS'. This could not be easier. Add up the amount of runs that the Batsmen have scored against the Bowler you are looking at and place the total in the Runs section. If he has bowled an over or overs without any runs being scored off him then that is a Maiden. If that happens, by the way, in his box for that over you will see you will end up with 6 dots, all you do is join them up with your pencil or pen to make a letter 'M', this a Maiden. Add up his Maidens and place the total in the box. In the Overs box count up and place in there the number of overs he has bowled. There has been no wicket taken in this innings so there is nothing to place in the WKTS box.

BROKEN CONCENTRATION

I fondly recall briefly losing concentration at a match being played by a club with which I was scoring.

Our captain, a giant of a man, was bowling and as he delivered the ball their striker hit it with ferocity. The ball sailed effortlessly into the ether, a term known as 'Coming down with snow on'.

As the ball climbed to an unbelievable height Robbo our fielder at the bowler's end, himself a superb fast bowler, was heard to exclaim 'How tall do you reckon that tree is then Jenno?', the ball having just cleared the summit of a particularly vast poplar tree. Jenno's reply was unprintable!

THOSE EXTRAS AGAIN!

Now go to the Extras section and add up all the extras and place them under the Batsmen's totals. Add the two together and that should equal your total of runs on your accumulative section, where you have been ticking off the runs one by one. The batting total, the accumulative total and the Bowlers' totals should all add up, the only difference is that byes and leg byes are not in the bowling analysis, you add them on in your head.

You are now ready for tea, well done and richly deserved! Let's not forget Scorers get a free tea, yippee!

RIGHT, LET'S GET DANGEROUS

You have now mastered the art of scoring at its basic level. Why don't we go one step further and add in the amount of balls that are faced by each Batsman in turn. So simple and nothing to concern you. You proceed as before except that every time the Batsman faces a ball, if he does not score from it, you simply put a dot in the section where you are scoring his runs. How superb is that? Now, at the end of his innings, you can tell him how many balls he has faced simply by counting them up. Also by looking at the time he went in to bat and the time he finished you can also count up the amount of minutes he was at the wicket. Many score books have sections for you to record these details. Even if they do not you can write them in along his batting analysis.

What happens if a wicket falls? This is where it can sometimes get tricky but don't worry, I am here to guide you through the morass that is:

THE DISMISSAL

Actually it could not be simpler. Do you remember when we totalled up the Batsmen's scores at the end of the innings there was a series of boxes marked with How Out, Bowler and Total? This is when they come into play. If the Batsman is Bowled, Caught, LBW or any other dismissal you simply put it down in the box that asks you How Out; don't forget that if he is caught you will need the name of the catcher here and the Wicketkeeper's name if he is stumped, etc. In the next box you put the name of the Bowler who has perpetrated the dastardly deed, finally his total. In the Batsmen's column where you have been adding up his scores you now draw a line or two lines to show he has finished. In the box of the Bowler the ball that dismissed him goes down as a small 'W'.

You are now ready for the next Batsman to come in.

THE RUN OUT

This is the same procedure for any dismissal except the infamous 'Run Out'. This is one of the most frustrating and at times comical dismissals on the field of play. It occurs when one Batsman runs but the other stays in his ground, if the running Batsman's wicket is then taken he is Run Out. Normally the one running is trying to boost up the total but at times it is the Striker who says 'No' too late to save his friend.

SORRY DAD

I recall one match when the opening pair were a father and son team. The son was on strike and his father was number 2. I heard the son call his father to run, which he did and then call 'No' which he did and during the next few seconds all I heard was the son shouting 'Yes, No, Yes, No, Sorry Dad!' as the father's wicket fell Run Out. The father stormed past me and said 'Third time this flaming season', I smiled gently and attempted to avoid wetting myself.

All you have to do with a Run Out is to mark in the How Out section exactly that 'Run Out', the Bowler does not get credit for the wicket, he does not get the small 'W' in his box, it stays a dot ball for the Bowler.

IT GETS BETTER

I think you are now ready to go one stage further. We have already seen how you join up the dots in the Bowler's box to make a 'M' when he has a maiden, why not do the same for the Batsman facing it? Writing very small, place a small 'm' in his column and that way you see how many Maidens each Batsman has faced.

SCORING BYES AND LEG BYES

You can even show Byes and Leg Byes in a similar way. (Actually do you think the plural of Leg Byes should be Legs Bye? It sounds so much nicer.) The MCC scoring guides allow you to show them in this way. A Bye is a small triangle point up, a Leg Bye is a small triangle point down. This is only a guideline and not hard and fast. I actually devised a method of my own many years ago. I show a square for a Leg Bye with the number of runs scored off it inside. Then for a Bye I use a diamond shape, again with the number of runs inside it. You can show these in the Batsman's column and in the Bowler's box. It's just another way of giving more information.

IS IT WORTH IT?

I have been asked by some of my colleagues why I make extra work for myself? The answer is simple. I believe that as a Scorer I must give as much information as possible to people viewing the book in the years to come.

It is however rather pleasant to see, over the years, other Scorers who have adopted some of my little tricks and now use them themselves. It's a great compliment and somewhat of a thrill to know that something you have worked on will live on long after I have joined the celestial gin distillery in the sky.

You will notice I have not mentioned the 'Scoreboard' yet, I was just lulling you into a false sense of security. Here it is now.

THE SCOREBOARD

Most boards at club level are simplicity itself, they just show Total Runs. Wickets. Overs. A series of numbers are placed either on hooks or slid onto runners at the end of each over to keep the board to date. It is sometimes called 'the Telegraph' by older cricketers.

GETTING HELP

If you are not near the board or are too busy please ask for help. The team who are waiting to bat should be only too willing to help. After all you are busy keeping the book. Remember that the book is vital, if you miss a ball whilst struggling with the board you may have an incorrect record of the game.

One hundred hundreds in a career

	Name	100s	Innings	Season
1.	J B Hobbs	199	1315	1923
2.	E H Hendren	170	1300	1928-9
3.	W R Hammond	167	1005	1935
4.	C P Mead	153	1340	1927
5.	G Boycott	151	1014	1977
6.	H Sutcliffe	157	1088	1932
7.	F E Woolley	145	1532	1929
8.	G A Hick	136	806	1998
9.	L Hutton	129	814	1951
10.	G A Gooch	128	990	1992-3

MECHANICAL BOXES

If your scoreboard is mechanical then it is even easier. The numbers are normally rotated into place by a series of pull strings with the numerals shown in mirror image in order that the ground observe the true score. Share the task with your fellow Scorer, take a string each, the job is soon done.

THE SCORER'S CONDUCT

Like your colleague the Umpire, you are a match official, yours is the duty of recording the game and forming an archive. Your work will survive long after the game is forgotten. If you have done a good job the record is permanent.

Behave as calmly as possible. At times, such as at a collapse of wickets when 3 or 4 players have been 'out' in as many minutes, try to stay collected. Nothing induces fear into the eyes of the Umpire as much as the vision of a deranged Scorer with a coloured pencil protruding from every orifice pulling frantically on the chords of the score box telegraph and resembling a manic string puppet. Stay in control, if you find yourself slipping behind switch to an ordinary pencil and scribble quick notes onto a plain paper pad, you can confer with it later.

A PLEASANT MEMORY

One club I attend used to have a charming lady Scorer who would, when she knew I was coming and the weather was warm, sit with me outside as we scored whilst sipping chilled wine and nibbling strawberries. Sheer bliss. Nadia I miss you!

Index

Index of TOP 10s

Please Note: All statistics stated in this book were correct at time of publication